Forward by Dr. John F. Kelly

The
CHANGING
Church
in the
UNCHANGING
Kingdom

Dr. Philip R. Byler

PUBLISHED BY PALM TREE PUBLICATIONS
A DIVISION OF PALM TREE PRODUCTIONS
KELLER, TEXAS U.S.A.
PRINTED IN THE U.S.A.

www.palmtreeproductions.net

Palm Tree Productions is a Media Services Company dedicated to seeing the Kingdom of God advanced by ministries and businesses with excellence, integrity and professionalism through the use of high quality media resources. Whether the publication is print, audio, or visual, we are dedicated to excellence in every aspect from concept to final production.

It is our desire that this publication will enrich your life and cause you to increase in wisdom and understanding.

For more information about products and services available through Palm Tree Productions, visit our website at www.palmtreeproductions.net.

THE CHANGING CHURCH IN THE UNCHANGING KINGDOM

Cover Photo: Big Stock Photos | Cover Design: Palm Tree Productions
Editor: Wendy K. Walters

ISBN:
978-0-9817054-0-8

LIBRARY OF CONGRESS CONTROL NUMBER:
2008925848

To contact the author, visit
WWW.CTTMMINISTRIES.COM

TABLE OF CONTENTS

V ACKNOWLEDGEMENTS

VII ENDORSEMENTS
—Dr. W. Paul "Buddy" Crum
—Dr. William Michael Comfort
—Jacquie Tyre

IX FORWARD
—Dr. John P. Kelly

XI PROLOGUE

Chapter One
1 New Vs. Old—
The Problem of Transition

Chapter Two
15 Change—
The Great Constant

Chapter Three
29 The Chaotic State
of The Institutional Church

Chapter Four
47 A Church Without Apostles

Chapter Five
67 Forming the Apostolic Community—
The Reemergence of The Apostolic

Chapter Six

89 APOSTOLIC THEOLOGY

Chapter Seven

107 THE CHURCH, THE KINGDOM,
APOSTLES, AND APOSTOLIC CHRISTIANITY

Chapter Eight

127 IDENTIFYING THE APOSTLES—
REDEFINING THE CHURCH

Chapter Nine

141 THE APOSTOLIC COMMUNITY AT WAR

Chapter Ten

161 KINGDOM CULTURE IN
THE APOSTOLIC COMMUNITY

181 APPENDIX

185 ABOUT THE AUTHOR

ACKNOWLEDGEMENTS

Space prevents me from acknowledging everyone who has brought me both inspiration and influence. I will not even try, but I will not forget you. Thank you for being a valued part of my life

I give praise to Almighty God—Father, Son, and Holy Spirit—for His faithfulness and constancy. He has sustained me through every trial of life. Like David of old, I have sought to know His ways more than His acts and that has made all the difference. That has made the message of the Kingdom as real as the Kingdom itself.

My wife, Dr. Judy Byler, has been my constant companion for more than forty-three years. She has walked faithfully by my side—encouraging, enduring, and praying me through. She is a partner in ministry and has courageously stood through every trial life has thrown our way. She has gone where I have gone, lodged where I have lodged, my people are her people, and my God, her God.

Our son, Timothy is seventh in the generational line of Christian ministry. He and his wife, Cindy, oversee Bethesda Church in Hinesville, GA, serving that church with integrity and zeal. We delight in their success and rejoice in their faithfulness. They have given us four amazing grandchildren—Heather, Josiah, Benjamin and Gracie Anne.

We further delight in our daughter Wendy. She, and her husband, Todd, own and operate Palm Tree Productions—and are publishers of this work. They bring a service to the body of Christ which is of tremendous value, providing for the success of Christian leaders through their professionalism, their dedication to excellence, and their commitment to Christ as leaders in the workplace. They have given us three more remarkable grandchildren—Kathryn, Emily and Joshua Philip, who carries my name.

I am deeply indebted to my dear friend, Dr. William Comfort, who stood with me through trying times as I was attempting to adapt to change, and who opened the door of opportunity by which I was able to obtain my doctorate. He and his wife have been faithful friends and supporters for many years.

I thank Apostle John Kelly for taking me into his world of ministry. In these later years of my life, I have been privileged to literally travel around the world with him. I have gleaned from his vast knowledge, drawn from the well of his anointing, and count him as both a friend and as my own apostolic overseer. He is amazing.

It is impossible to name all of the life contributors who have shaped and molded my perspectives. Congregations I have served, influential people who have given me voice and challenge, a wide variety of preachers, teachers, and Christian writers, who through their words created a hunger and a thirst for God's glory to be manifested in me.

Finally, I want to express my deep and abiding love and honor for my father, Samuel E. Byler. He served the Lord unrelentingly for the final sixty-three years of his life. His commitment to the Word of God and his dedication to reaching people both inspired me and challenged me as I entered into Christian ministry as my life's profession. I stand upon his shoulders, reaching to expand the Kingdom of God beyond the sphere to which he was limited. If he had lived in this age, he would have been recognized as an apostle. He was, though he never really knew it to be so.

—Dr. Philip R. Byler

ENDORSEMENTS

Dr. Byler has given the reader a comprehensive but uncomplicated presentation of the progression of the Kingdom through the Apostolic perspective. He has wisely shown that transformation occurs when the apostolic is actively involved in the leadership of changing the church and expressing the Kingdom. It gives hope and excitement for the body of Christ that we really will see the Glory of the Lord become perfected against the Kingdom of darkness.

This book is instrumental in understanding the apostolic as a main catalyst for the new covenant church perspective. It is a primer for those desiring to have a full understanding of the apostolic.

—Dr. W. Paul "Buddy" Crum, Apostle
Co-Senior Pastor, Life Center Family Church
Director of Life Center Ministries, Inc.
Christian International Ministries, Board of Governors
Dunwoody, Georgia

There is a shift of gigantic proportions taking place today throughout the worldwide body of Christ. Dead liturgical churches throughout western Europe are museum attractions of the past which tourists now rarely even visit. Theologically liberal churches in North America are struggling to even exist. Yet, on the other hand, Bible teaching, Spirit-filled churches throughout Asia, Africa, Latin America, and North America are filled with people celebrating the love of the Lord Jesus Christ. Emerging from this great modern day revival is the New Apostolic Reformation. Dr. Philip R. Byler's book, THE CHANGING CHURCH IN THE UNCHANGING KINGDOM could not have come at a better time. This vital book has laid the ground work for the reproduction of Apostolic men and women to provide leadership that ensures the continual growth of our mighty present day revival.

Dr. Byler proves in his book that this is already taking place and also provides the plan of how to keep it going. Once you begin to read this book, you won't want to stop until you read it through.

—Dr. William Michael Comfort,
President and Founder of Chesapeake Bible College & Seminary
Ridgely, Maryland

In this age of the New Apostolic Reformation, it is important that we have men and women to help establish strong moorings to anchor us in the midst of times of "being tossed to and fro by every wind of doctrine" that rises in the midst of new moves of God. Dr. Phil, as we affectionately know him, brings together Biblical truth with historical church history. He adds to this practical, contemporary experience woven in to form a three-stranded cord that cannot easily be broken or frayed. His style of communication is engaging, his honest transparency challenging, and his poignant ways of uncovering areas of inconsistency (or even error) that riddle the way we "do church"—convicting.

Prepare to be challenged. Prepare to think. Prepare to change. Prepare to understand in a new way. And, prepare to be a part of the apostolic church rising in our generation to "go and make disciples of all nations."

—Jacquie Tyre. Apostle
President, Kairos Transformation Ministries
Chancellor, Wagner Leadership Institute-Southeast
Lilburn, Georgia

FORWARD

The message of the Kingdom of God is not just a teaching for the early church, it is relevant and necessary to all believers in Christ today. Jesus spoke about the Kingdom of God more than any other topic. Jesus taught it, used it, developed it, and functioned in it to transform His disciples. It was to be their way. To them it was the way—the only way that they were to live, and move, and have their being. These disciples moved in a particular, principled, and unifying way to build His Kingdom—each using different gifts, talents, and assignments to do so.

The early church was discipled not to be revivalists, but to be revolutionists. Their calling and training was to establish a spiritual army of a peculiar kind of people that would become prayer warriors, intercessors, and witnesses of a King of love and power. They were to establish this Kingdom by penetrating all levels of society and culture. They were to reach slaves, tradesmen, merchants, money lenders, tax collectors, soldiers, politicians, gladiators...you name it. They were to reach the extremely wealthy as well as the extremely poor. The plan was simply to reach out to those they were in relationship with in the workplace and in the marketplace—regardless of whether they were their bosses, their peers, or slaves and servants.

The early church reached and changed the cultures of much of the known world at this time. It touched and transformed cities, and had a profound effect upon them as a counter-cultural force. It stood against the culture of the Roman Empire, the Grecian Empire, the Mesopotamian and Phoenician Empires—and did so without modern systems of communication and transportation. The call to the early church was to be a force in power.

Whatever station in life they were in, whatever duties they performed, whatever responsibilities were theirs, they did them in a more excellent way.

The plan was simple. It was to make disciples in all economic, racial, and social realms. When these disciples came together they became the church (the *ecclesia*). From then until now, the desire of the church is to be relevant, revelational, and most of all, revolutional. As the early church was, the contemporary church must remain counter-cultural—it is to be a model and a reflection of the Godhead. The church is constantly changing, regenerating, re-birthing, and re-establishing itself.

There are certain things that God has restored to the church that will remain. There are other things that are incidentals—only in place for a time or season. If we're to go from glory to glory, then we must also go from season to season, from change to change. Local church government must be open to change and must be led of the Holy Spirit. It must be flexible, movable, and adaptable.

In this book, *The Changing Church in the Unchanging Kingdom*, you will discover dynamic truths and principles to bring the church through the coming change to strengthen the unchanging Kingdom. Dr. Phil Byler explains the past, present, and future in a way that is clear and insightful. This is a must read book for all Christians and Christian leaders.

—Dr. John P. Kelly
CEO, Leadership Education for Apostolic Development (LEAD)
CEO, International Christian WealthBuilders℠ Foundation (ICWBF)
Ambassador Apostle, International Coalition of Apostles (ICA)

PROLOGUE

The tall, lanky preacher paced back and forth across the platform like a caged tiger. It was almost as though he wanted to step across the edge of the platform and wade into the audience to make his point. He spoke with a deep, "aw shucks" kind of Carolina accent and an abandonment of proper language that simply drew you in and held your attention. He was so animated and intense that it was impossible not to listen. His point was this, "The Kingdom of God is here, it is manifested, and it is love." His name was Tommy Lewis. Though he never went past the ninth grade in school, he had a profound perception of the Kingdom of God. He spoke to my soul, and I was hooked forever.

I am one of those proverbial "raised in church" kids. My father was a preacher, and I can never remember a time when Christianity and church were not a part of my life. I accepted Jesus Christ as my Lord and Savior when I was just six years old, and embraced a call to ministry when I was fourteen. Oh, I had a few tempestuous years, when I "fled to Tarshish," but the reality and validity of my Christian faith has never really been much of an issue. Still, I did not understand the Kingdom of God. To me, it was merely another way of saying heaven. Then I met Tommy, and things began to change.

That was in 1973, and it was during that summer that I embraced Matthew 6:33 as my life verse: "Seek ye first the Kingdom of God and His righteousness, and all these things shall be added unto you." I'll readily admit that I have not always allowed this challenge to guide my steps. But, it has always brought me back to center. When I drifted away in my pursuit of life—the Kingdom brought me back. When I tried to move into theological deep water that had no life transformation—the Kingdom brought me back. It has been the Kingdom, and the ever present, never changing righteousness of Jesus Christ that always has drawn me back to the Master's side, yielded to His Lordship and committed to His service.

Over the course of time, I have listened to countless preachers try to expound and explain the Kingdom. Some get it, some don't. Most try to mesh the Kingdom and the church into a single entity. From that perspective, everything that happens in the Kingdom must occur within the church, and vice versa. Our ongoing delusion that the church and the Kingdom are one and the same thing tends to limit our capacity to extend the reach of the Kingdom into the world. Standard practice is to try to bring the world into the church for an "extreme makeover." This has proven to be an inefficient, ineffective process of cultural transformation. It is costly in terms of personnel, time, and money. The problem is rather simple—we need to stop trying to squeeze the world into a church-shaped box.

Given time, the church will change. It has in the past, it will in the future. The Kingdom, however, is unshakable and unchanging. It has been and will continue to be exactly what it has always been—the reign of God. It will not only be the reign of God, it will be the loving reign of the loving God. He rules, not simply by Divine decree. He rules with compassion and grace, with dignity and honor, with love and mercy, with justice and with truth. When we, if we who make up the Christian community ever truly understand that things will change. We will be better equipped to establish His dominion in our world. But as long as we continue with a "church as usual" mentality, we will continue to experience little more than what we currently see happening.

People will come and people will go. Some church communities will grow while others will cease to exist. The church is not going to go away. It may simply become irrelevant unless it makes some dramatic changes. In the past, God has used the great periods of reformation and transformation, and the tremendous dedication of countless saints to pre-serve, maintain, and even expand the church. In the process, the Kingdom has not changed at all. It remains the Kingdom of our Lord and of His Christ.

At this writing, we are engaged in another time of trans-formation, one that some are calling a new reformation. Technically, they are calling it the New Apostolic Reforma-tion. I have joined that company in full confidence that God has restored a growing awareness and acknowledgement of the apostolic to His church. Systematically, over the past half-century or so, He has validated and empowered thousands of individuals with fresh understanding of His Kingdom and a willingness to embrace a position within the five-fold min-istry structure Paul addressed in Ephesians, chapter four.

Unfortunately, with this time of restoration has come a host of title seekers, position grabbers, and ill-prepared novices who have laid claim to something they have not been fully equipped to do. These ministry gifts/offices are not given for personal aggrandizement, power posturing, or professional elevation. They are given to the body of Christ for the single purpose of properly and adequately preparing the body to expand Kingdom influence and power into the world.

This book addresses this challenge and one other, perhaps a more significant one. For the past "umpteen" hundred years, the church has accepted its role as being an aside from the daily life and experience of common people. Church organizations, denominations, buildings, and institutions have erected what I can only label as a "stained glass wall" of separation between the secular and the sacred. Like the renowned "iron and bamboo curtains" that isolated and insulated the communist world from an enterprising world, so the "stained glass wall" isolates the church. That wall must be dismantled, broken, shattered. It must be replaced by a contemporary apostolic infrastructure that is responsive to

Holy Spirit and conscious of an elevated role of influence in a world gone mad.

The Changing Church in the Unchanging Kingdom is, more than anything else, a book of observations and conclusions based on more than thirty-five years of ministry. Most of that was spent behind that barrier of "stained glass." Only in the latter years did I come to realize the utter necessity of removing that barrier beyond mere rhetoric. Today, the contemporary apostolic movement is doing just that, but an entrenched mindset does not dissipate easily. Much instruction, a growing level of insight, and a broadening bibliography of apostolically inclined literature will only partially solve the problem. We must become apostolic as Christians, promoting and engaging in an effective, intentional discipleship process.

Being apostolic or apostolically minded is a far cry from being an apostle. Using the word apostle or apostolic neither validates a call nor qualifies an individual for a position of responsible ministry. Yet, being apostolically minded is vitally important to every believer. We are called and sent as the body of Christ, to manifest His presence in our lives through every situation of life. This is not a church mandate—it is a Kingdom mandate. The church will change. Indeed, the church must change. But the Kingdom will remain, and will continue to be.

As you read and study this book, I pray that you will be challenged to rise to a new level of commitment to be sent. Your generation needs you. Your workplace needs you. The people in whom you delight and the places they haunt need you. They need you, not as a titled minister of the church, but as an apostolically-inclined, sent by God representative of Jesus Himself. They need you because you bring the Kingdom.

—Dr. Philip R. Byler
March 2008
Atlanta, Georgia

CHAPTER
1

NEW VS. OLD—
THE PROBLEM OF
TRANSITION

Every unfolding move of God meets resistance. Each transition the church goes through creates a set of dynamics that seems to repeat itself. Perhaps the 'old wineskin/new wineskin' paradigm that Jesus spoke of will always apply.[1] The more institutionalized the church becomes, the harder it is to embrace new ideas and fresh perspectives. Religion ever seeks to develop and maintain ritual and tradition as a means of maintaining continuity and stability. New movements seem to always resist at least some rituals and traditions. Thus, the emerging church is in conflict with the established church. The emerging church moves forward. The established church resists. We desperately need a fresh move of God.

Usually within the established church there are forward looking people. These, along with new believers who are not yet immobilized by tradition and ritual, and those who have long been frustrated with the "baggage" of institution, move on. They form new cells and congregations. Either that or they become part of newly formed congregations of the new movement. Unfortunately, in doing this they bring with them a residue of the old paradigm—"leaven." If not purged out this residue will simply begin to "leaven the whole lump."[2] With the passing of time, the new becomes old, stagnates and becomes stale, and God again has to blow a fresh wind of the Spirit across the church.

This has been the fate of so many of the marvelous moves of God over the centuries. Once vibrant, enthusiastic and passionate, they take on airs of spiritual superiority. Their leaders often grow self-assured and aloof. They cease to be forward looking. They resist change and withstand creative, innovative input. In most cases, they fail to raise up and release new leadership, thus they eventually lock themselves into a mindset that becomes rigid and unyielding. An unnoticed, un-addressed arrogance seeps into the fabric of faith. It is a certain precursor to disaster.[3]

This will be the fate of the New Apostolic Reformation we are now experiencing unless we embrace the apostolic as a reality that must be reproduced on a continuing basis. Disciples must be apostolic and apostolic disciples must raise up disciples who also become apostolic. They must train them and then release them to experience and express the ever expanding revelation of God's purpose, power, and grace. They must prepare them to be qualified in their lives and character. From this band of apostolic disciples, Jesus will select and appoint more apostles.

THE DECLINE OF PAST MOVES OF GOD

The decline of every major move of God can be traced directly to a failure to sustain a discipleship mandate. Forward thinking, innovative, and insightful apostolic men and women were at the vanguard of those mighty moves. Disciples gathered around them—people who believed, embraced, and assisted in the rapid propagation of the truth they saw. As those movements grew and took on momentum, cells and congregations developed, often forming denominations or forming groups that functioned like denominations in the process. Because of their passion and zeal, these disciples easily drew others around them. As long as a spiritual movement made more disciples than it lost, the movement grew and was sustained. However, when the movement stopped making disciples institutionalism set in. Or perhaps when institutionalism set in, they simply stopped making and started losing disciples.

> THE DECLINE OF EVERY MAJOR MOVE OF GOD CAN BE TRACED DIRECTLY TO A FAILURE TO SUSTAIN A DISCIPLESHIP MANDATE.

The apostolic call may be expressed in numerous ways. In fact, this has been the case. Numerous highly qualified and spiritually astute communicators have written in detail regarding the ministry, call, and anointing of apostles. Their insight reveals that one of the key elements of apostolic ministry and life is the reproductive nature of apostles. As primary leaders in Christianity, apostles have a responsibility to reproduce themselves many times over. They are to train, equip, release, and send resourceful, insightful men and women into apostolic ministry.

These new apostolic disciples must be willing to be creative and innovative, open to the leading of the Holy Spirit. They must be willing to remain connected with and lovingly submitted to their own apostolic fathers. They are not to be clones, to be sure, but they will be marked with the spiritual "DNA" of the one who has been set by God to prepare, disciple, train, and send them. This and this alone will sustain the ongoing nature of apostolic life, of Divine government, and of Kingdom expansion.

LOSING DISCIPLES

Disciples are lost to the Kingdom in two ways. The first is obvious. They leave and go elsewhere. They sail in on a fresh wind of the Spirit, are blown aside by winds of adversity, and finally drop out of the church. All too often fledgling apostles and committed disciples become dispirited or weary from being used or abused without being developed and released. They have a genuine call from God—a sense of their purpose and calling. Without being developed in God, they eventually realize they will never be sent. Their choice is to break the ties of personal loyalty in favor of finding a destiny that is fulfilling. This is a very difficult thing, both for the mentor and for the disciple. The break is often tainted with hurt feelings and harsh words. It is sad, but it could be remedied by a better standard of training and releasing God-called men and women into ministry.

Vibrant and active disciples are also lost to the movement because they lose interest. Poorly developed or weak relationships, coupled with high demands on personal energy, time, and resources are often culprits that reduce vibrant faith to nominal adherence. High expectations of performance without correspondingly returned commitment result in a huge letdown for many. Things outside the faith begin to attract people's interest and skills. Approval, appreciation, and a sense that their contribution is important by individuals, organizations, and enterprises outside the church draw them away.

Without a sense of truly belonging, they easily drift toward pleasure seeking or personal business endeavors. All too often, they form frivolous, meaningless, or harmful relationships that draw them away from God's call. This is sad, because they are not only lost to a movement, they are lost to Kingdom effectiveness.

The second way that disciples are lost to a movement is not so obvious, though it may be more destructive. These disciples simply stop being disciples. They don't leave, but they only remain as followers. They believe, but they cease to act on their beliefs. They just stop making disciples.

They stop propagating the truth they believe. In other words, they cease to be apostolic, or sent. Instead they are content to gather periodically, once or twice a week, in "sheepfolds" called churches. They sometimes encourage their flagging spirituality with conferences on faith or works, deeper-life weekends, or revival meetings. They convince themselves that they are doing the work of the Lord. In that sense, perhaps, they are fulfilling Jesus' words to Peter "feed my sheep."[4] But that is all they are doing, feeding sheep. They are not making disciples. The work of disciple making gets relegated to professional ministers, program administrators, and new believers.

> **MAKING DISCIPLES MUST BE ETCHED INTO OUR SPIRITUAL DNA.**

A genuinely apostolic community cannot function that way. The mandate of the Great Commission is a clarion call to the truly apostolic church. Making disciples must be etched into our spiritual DNA. Every congregation and every cell of the church, if it is to be apostolic in nature, must become intentional in the pursuit of making disciples. It must be engraved in our thinking and etched upon our hearts.

Institutionalized Stability— The Church We Have Received

This lack of a concentrated discipleship mentality has resulted in a church of forms and formalities. Instead of focusing on the development of reproductive disciples, we have focused on developing everything else. At one end of the spectrum, some people are content to develop small, closely-knit relational groups. They gather in cloisters of self-realization and self-fulfillment, pursuing a spiritual idealism. These are often comprised of individuals who have had all the "church as usual" stuff they can take. Yet, they do not want to give up on their faith. Making entrance into such groups (and hence into the Kingdom) is a bit difficult because added numbers create added organizational necessities.

At the other end of the spectrum are congregations rapidly increasing in size where spiritual anonymity can be achieved with relative ease. Church facilities grow ever larger and more elaborate. Times of corporate worship are filled with inspiring sight and sound. Sermons are often little more than motivational syrup or prosperity promises.

A host of stimulating programs has been created for children, youth and "tweeners" who act as though they have not reached an age of accountability. "Golden-agers" are increasingly entertained as though they had passed the age of reliability. Much creativity, wisdom, and effective ministry is lost because these groups are ministered to rather than trained, equipped, and empowered as ministers. The productive core of such churches primarily lies

7

somewhere between the two extremes. Predominantly young and middle aged adult congregants are hard pressed to balance the various challenges of family, employment, spiritual activity and personal fulfillment.

In facing the challenges of meeting or ministering to the needs (or the felt needs) of everyone, these churches have little choice but to organize into an institutional culture of programs, meetings, and church directed opportunities. Now mind you, programs can be quite good. But they are not necessarily Kingdom. They are primarily designed to meet the needs or supposed needs of people. In other words, programs are designed to *be* ministry, not to train ministers to *do* ministry. They do not usually produce effective disciples who are equipped to make disciples.

> **PROGRAMS LEAD TO INSTITUTIONALIZED THINKING AS SURELY AS INSTITUTIONALIZED THINKING LEADS TO PROGRAMS.**

I am not suggesting that better discipleship programs need to be instituted. Far from it. Programs lead to institutionalized thinking as surely as institutionalized thinking leads to programs.

Programs can easily become protected territory—provinces of personal achievement that prevent discipleship from occurring. When this occurs personal transformation can be missed as the ones being discipled strive to meet the demands of curriculum.

A More Productive Discipleship Model

True discipleship must go beyond the limitations of curriculum alone. Discipleship must be focused on the development of lives. It occurs more effectively through dynamic relationships than it does though formal training. Disciple makers need to be sensitive to the "teachable moments" that occur in their relationships with emerging disciples. They must seize them and use them to coach, teach, train, and mentor emerging disciples.

Discipleship is a process that reinforces the emerging disciple's relationship with Jesus through a vital relationship with the disciple maker. God does not intend for us to make disciples of ourselves, our teachings, or our personal values. We are to make disciples of Jesus Christ. Our teachings, our values, and our insights must reflect the heart and mind of Christ if we are to successfully mentor others and make them disciples.

One of the mistakes of the past has been to try to make disciples of ourselves. Paul's statements, "imitate me," and "follow me as I follow Christ."[5] should sound an alarm in the heart of every apostolic man or woman who desires to lead others. No one has the right to call anyone else to follow him or her, unless his or her own discipleship is stalwart and sincere. Character is at the pinnacle of apostolic requirements. This is a problem every disciple maker will face. None of us is wholly above reproach. We could all be impeached in some area, but the model must stand strong and sure.

Apostolic discipleship is always aware of the personal connection encouraged by the words, "follow me." But disciple makers must understand their own vulnerability and fallibility as mentors. People duplicate those things that are modeled to them. They do what they see and hear. Or, at least they try to do what they see and hear. So it is important that the disciple maker prevent the emerging disciple from duplicating flaws in his own life and ministry.

> **PEOPLE DUPLICATE THOSE THINGS THAT ARE MODELED TO THEM.**

People must be mentored in what not to do as well as in what to do. The model is Jesus.[6] He is the example that disciples are to model their lives after. We must be full of grace and faith, filled with the Holy Spirit, and determined to follow His lead.

JESUS' METHOD OF DISCIPLESHIP

Jesus' method was first to do, then to explain, and finally to use a scenario that would cause His disciples to put into practice what they had seen and heard. Behind practically every miracle, a Kingdom principle was revealed. Every parable was the veneer of a much deeper truth. Disciple makers will, of necessity, uncover the deeper truths of the Kingdom for those emerging disciples who are being trained by them. The exhortation to the disciple may well be, "follow me." The cry from the heart of the sincere disciple is, "mentor me."

> THE CRY FROM THE HEART OF THE SINCERE DISCIPLE IS, "MENTOR ME."

Embracing the apostolic requires that ministry equippers be developed. The disciple maker will always be an apostolic person. That does not mean he or she will be an apostle with a title and a broad-based sphere of spiritual government. Being apostolic means that the disciple maker will be conscious of his or her role to coach, teach, train, and mentor those emerging disciples who are in their own sphere. Out of this band of "fully functional followers of Jesus Christ," gifted apostles will emerge. They will become known through;

+ the anointing that will become apparent on their lives;

+ an ever-widening sphere of influence that governs the direction of church life;

+ taking on the fathering role (gender non-specific) in Kingdom affairs—leading, directing, commissioning, and releasing well-discipled disciple makers into areas of ministry.

Apostles will be discontented with institutional situations, meaningless ritual, and caustic leadership. They will be confident and spiritually empowered visionaries and builders. And, apostles will be relational to the core.

WHO ARE THE DISCIPLES—REALLY?

Apostles will make disciples who will be disciple makers. Disciple makers will make disciples who will be disciple makers. And out of those disciple makers, new apostles will emerge. They may come from the ranks of pastors, evangelists, teachers, and even prophets. They will just as likely come from the ranks of doctors, bankers, farmers, and mechanics. They might be politicians, business executives, or restaurateurs. They may serve in the military, on police forces, or as educators. The role of the church is being defined by a resurgence of ministry in the workplace. The realization that the real impact of the Kingdom of God is outside the walls of the church has become a hallmark of the future. As individual churches and leaders embrace the apostolic, they will in all probability lose their impact as institutions or as

> THE REAL IMPACT OF THE KINGDOM OF GOD IS OUTSIDE THE WALLS OF THE CHURCH.

institutional leaders. Instead, they will become agents of change through the dynamic influence of their apostolic stance in the culture of the community of which they are a part.

Around the world the Kingdom is advancing. Multiplied thousands of people are responding to the message of the Bible daily. As they do, they are forming thousands of churches and Christian communities. Amazingly, they are quite similar in form and function to the church described in the book of Acts. In other words, they are Pentecostal in fervor, zealously evangelistic, and apostolic in their biblical perspective. It is the established church, not the developing one that has a problem making the transition. God is setting things in order. He is restoring the church to the pattern He established in its earliest days. The question is: are we ready and willing to embrace what He is doing? Are we ready for change?

DISCUSSION QUESTIONS

✦ In what ways can you see the institutional nature of the church preventing effective discipleship?

✦ What are some of the felt needs of people that are being met by some program(s) you are involved in?

✦ What could be done to empower that program or "ministry" to become more effective as an equipping experience for people rather than being a needs meeting experience?

✦ What was the pattern of discipleship Jesus modeled?

✦ How will emerging apostles become known?

CHAPTER
2

CHANGE—THE GREAT CONSTANT

Change happens. This is the nature of all things created. Animal, vegetable or mineral, all things in creation change. This is the nature of life. Only God and His Kingdom remain unchanged, unmoved and immovable. He is the Great Constant, the Eternal and Supreme of all Creation. Through Him, all things were created and have their being.[1] His eternal nature and His unchanging attributes are the substance upon which we base our faith and embrace a stable and just morality.

God's way is perfect.[2] It is not subject to the manipulations of a self-serving and unrepentant humanity. Still, the biblical record indicates that He has changed His mind or the course of His actions from time to time. Rest assured this is not a whimsical act on His part. He is not fickle and subject to impulsive behavior. He is God—omnipotent, omnipresent, omniscient God.

God is not subject to corruption, decay, or deterioration. Mankind is. When God changes, He does so because He chooses the change. Change doesn't choose Him. Not so for us humans. We are subject to the limitations imposed by the curse. We do grow old and feeble. We decay. And with every breath we draw, we must reckon with change. For us, change is irresistible. It is undeniable and gradual—almost indistinguishable. Nevertheless, change happens.

> WHEN THINGS CEASE TO CHANGE, THEY CEASE TO GROW. BUT EVEN WHEN THEY CEASE TO GROW, THEY DO NOT CEASE TO CHANGE.

Everything from rock formations to plants change as they grow. Children change as they grow. So do organizations and institutions. As my friend, Dr. Dean Radtke often says, "growth without change is impossible." It makes sense. When things cease to change, they cease to grow. But even when they cease to grow, they do not cease to change. They deteriorate. They rot, or they crystallize. In other words, change without growth is decay. Simply put, change is inevitable.

Markets change. Companies change. Institutions and entities change. Technologies change. Nations change. But the nature of God, His righteousness, His justice, His mercy, and His love never changes. These are immutable attributes of His character and persona. Societies and cultures function best where they concur with God's nature and embrace His righteousness. Where they violate that nature, they deteriorate into horrible chaos.

Infrastructures must constantly be redesigned to accommodate a constantly changing work environment. Rules must be evaluated and often rewritten to adapt to the shifting perspectives and needs of society and culture. Education must adapt to an ever broadening body of knowledge. Time passes, taking no heed to those of us who would like to slow its pace or reverse its course. As it does, change happens; sometimes for the better, sometimes not.

MANAGING CHANGE

The practical response to change, then, is to work with it, not against it. If everything is changing, the wise thing would be to embrace change and use it to our advantage. Far too often, by resisting change, people try to adjust God's design and reorder His purpose. This is both impractical and unreasonable.

We must learn to manage change. More precisely, we must learn to manage our responses to change. Rather than ineffectively try to force everything around us to change, we must embrace change and use it to our advantage. We must change with change—allow

> **WE MUST CHANGE WITH CHANGE— ALLOW IT TO BE A FRIEND RATHER THAN A FOE.**

it to be a friend rather than a foe. By failing to manage change, we fall into the trap of being dominated and controlled. Our circumstances then govern our reactions and responses, and we fall into the snare of an enemy who uses our resistance to change to dominate our lives, govern our circumstances, and limit our potential.

Most people resist change. They expect that change will not really affect them. But change always happens, and when it does, it forces people to adapt, even when they are unprepared to do so. Often, they react in ways that are non-productive and fail to foster growth. Instead of things improving, they deteriorate. This is true of the church as a whole as well as it is for individuals.

Since its earliest days, the history of the Christian church has been a history of change. The new believers in the emerging Christian community, faced with the promise and power of the New Covenant, were propelled into tremendous change. Birthed out of the sacrificial system of ancient Judaism, the early Christians were faced with serious crises of transition. True, they were filled with delight because of the life that flowed through their hearts. They enthusiastically and rapidly spread the joy they had, ushering multiplied thousands into the Kingdom of God. But from the church's very beginning it was beset with difficult choices and challenging predicaments. Even before the times of great persecution came upon the church, they found themselves facing problems.

CHANGE IN SOME PRESENTS GREAT CHALLENGES TO OTHERS

For instance, we know that to some degree, the experience of the early church was constantly marked by supernatural occurrences. True, the apostles gathered together the rapidly growing community of believers. Every day they were in the temple teaching. The believers extended themselves in acts of hospitality. They ate together. They prayed together. They even shared their possessions so that no one among them would suffer lack.[3] And they did this without committees or church boards.

Such a notable spirit of generous sharing must surely have generated interest and admiration. Quite probably, it also fostered a measure of acclaim. It also activated a spirit of greed that manifested in Annanias and Sapphira. Without question, the dishonesty of these two believers, and God's stunning response was dramatic and severe. For the whole body of believers, their deaths must have been terribly unsettling and fear-provoking.[4] After that, no one took their faith responses lightly for a long, long time.

The dishonesty of Annanias and Sapphira may seem trite to our way of thinking. To the early church it was a totally unacceptable breach of faith. Their deaths have served as examples to the whole body of Christ for millennia.

Ananias and Sapphira were not the only early disciples who had to be dealt with for some moral breakdown. In several instances we read of sinful actions and words of

19

correction that had to be delivered. However, the severity of the punishment in regard to these two struck a compelling note of fear in the early church community that has never completely dissipated. Lying to the Holy Ghost is not wise.

LYING TO THE HOLY GHOST IS NOT WISE.

As we study the New Testament, we note that the apostles had to impose specific moral requirements on the newly forming church. To our church-defined, contemporary, moral perspective, the imposition of obvious moral specifics seems rudimentary. We should remember, however, that although the early Christians were primarily Jewish, the growing church rapidly grafted in a Gentile component. The concept of morality within pagan religions is a far cry from that contained within the Bible. To bring such morally challenged people into the newly forming church had to have been stressful. Any truly evangelistic contemporary church can testify to the re-socialization that must occur when an unbeliever is brought into a Christian experience. Biblical morality does not automatically occur at the moment of salvation. Would that this were true. But most of us can testify to the challenges we face from time to time, living within the boundaries of our faith.

Acts chapter six records another major problem—one of prejudice and unjust treatment toward one group by another. Believers with Hebraic backgrounds from Jerusalem and surrounding areas held significant prejudice against believers with Greek backgrounds. These were people who had become a part of the church in Jerusalem, but they had been raised throughout the Greek and Roman world in communities much more closely related to Greek culture and custom. These were called Hellenistic Jews and the prejudices against them were not dissimilar to those held against the Samaritans.

This generated a most difficult situation, requiring special attention. The apostles' response was to appoint a group of administrative overseers.[5] These seven men are often identified as deacons in the church today, but they were not really deacons. Neither were they ordinary men. They were men of exceptional character who had the full allegiance both of the apostles and the growing congregation.

YOUR CHANGE MAY NOT BE ACCEPTABLE TO THOSE AROUND YOU

Jewish outrage and persecution surrounded the early Christian community to such a degree that they were scattered across the known world.[6] As they scattered, persecution increased. Furthermore, Roman persecution soon overshadowed Jewish persecution in a substantial way. History records wide spread, vicious persecution of Christians that continued through the beginning of the fourth century A.D. Instead of crushing Christianity, however, persecution served to spread it throughout the Roman empire. Unquenchable zeal and burning passion accompanied these early saints, and as they scattered across the Empire, they carried the message of the transforming power that came through trusting in the Risen Christ.

This early history of the church is often reported in Sunday Schools and Bible classes. It is a subject that receives a great deal of attention, especially as it applies to the Apostle Paul. He was one of the notable prosecutors of the persecution prior to his conversion. Even after he was converted, a significant amount of time passed before he was accepted in the community of believers. His reputation as a persecutor of the church was known far and wide. So terrible was his reputation that most believers were unwilling to embrace this militant tyrant following his conversion. But a few did, and eventually, he became a driving force and an articulate voice within the Christian movement.

It was Paul the Apostle who, more than any other writer, detailed the nature and structure of the early church. It was Paul who took the message of the Gospel to the far reaches of the empire. Teaming together, first with Barnabas and later with Silas, Paul traveled across the whole Mediterranean region spreading the Gospel. God used his insights and writings to communicate a significant portion of Christian theology, doctrine, and church order. He is quoted and referenced throughout the Christian community with a certainty of authority second only to Jesus Christ. His words are accepted as inspired by the Holy Ghost, and his position among the biblical characters is second to none, not even Moses.

Biblical evidence, as well as extra-biblical sources and tradition tell us that the other apostles traveled far and wide with the message of Christ's redemption as well. The first apostolic period was an age of expansion, transition, and development of the church. Most church historians indicate that the Gospel penetrated the entire known world in less than one generation following the ascension of Jesus Christ. In at least three places, Romans 1:8; Romans 10:18; and Colossians 1:6, the apostle Paul indicates this to be true.

Outlawed by Roman emperors, banned in the prevailing culture, hunted down, imprisoned, persecuted, tortured, and often martyred for the faith they held—this was early Christianity. The church of today is a far cry from the church of the first and second centuries. Across some two thousand years of church history, numerous sweeping and dramatic changes have occurred—changes that affect practically every aspect of Christian experience and thought.

THE CHURCH WE HAVE RECEIVED

Little remains that can truly be traced back to first century practice. The way we govern our churches is different. The conduct of our worship services is very different. The locations where we meet are very different. We are inundated with Sunday school classes, training seminars, recovery and special interest groups. Instead of perceiving the church as a collective, geographical entity, each city, town, village, and hamlet has numerous local and usually disconnected congregations. Each has some exclusive perspective that identifies it from others. Each has its own leadership, its own governmental protocols, its own way of doing things, and its own highly doctrinalized literature.

In many instances, the very core of Christian beliefs regarding the nature of redemption has been adapted to denominational standards or some biased theological perspective. Two thousand years of Christian history have seen changes of remarkable consequence—and not all of them were good by any means.

The vast bibliography of literature and research testifies to a multitude of transitions the church has endured. The historical record does not lack in uncovering these transitions. There are histories of the great Ecumenical councils, histories of the rise of the papacy, and histories of the schisms of the church. There is significant documentation of the dark ages of Western history, of the Protestant Reformation, and the rise of the modern church. All these woven together tell the story of our faith, its development, its strengths, its weaknesses, and its survival. But, the most notable fact regarding the church through its history has received little

> **THE MOST NOTABLE FACT REGARDING THE CHURCH— THE APOSTOLIC CHARACTER OF THE CHURCH WAS, FOR ALL PRACTICAL PURPOSES, EXTINGUISHED.**

attention. The apostolic character of the church was, for all practical purposes, extinguished.

The form and function of the church Jesus established was buried under a mountain of religious structure, tradition, and humanly engineered dogma.

21ST CENTURY APOSTOLIC RESTORATION

From the time of Jesus until the challenge of the distribution of goods in Acts 6, the only officials in the church were apostles. At the beginning, the church had no pastors, no elders, no bishops. None of our modern ecclesiastical structure was present in the earliest days of Christianity—just apostles.

These leaders were the select men Jesus had chosen and trained for the three and one-half years of His earthly ministry. Eleven of them had been appointed by Him while He was with them. A twelfth, Judas Iscariot (who betrayed Jesus), was replaced by Matthias, who was selected by lot from among those who had been disciples all along. Their specific task had been simply stated by Jesus before He ascended into heaven—make disciples.[7]

Who but God could have predicted the immediate, rapid growth of the church? From the day of Pentecost forward, Luke, in the book of Acts, records a rate of growth that staggers the modern mind.

Now, in the early days of the 21st century, reports from around the world announce that this kind of explosive growth is once again taking place. In many places it is being manifested, primarily in contemporary apostolic communities in the third world and the developing world. These communities value cooperation and interdependence. They are unencumbered by institution and tradition. They embrace the obviously apostolic nature of the New Testament message and of apostolic leadership and practice. They are communities that are willing to embrace change.

People are being drawn into the Kingdom of God by the thousands every day. In Africa, Asia, and South America, Christian expansion is huge. In the United States, however, this phenomenal growth has scarcely registered within the conventional settings of institutional church structures and mission organizations. Most church growth here is little more than people changing places, moving from one institution to another. The net growth of the church in the United States has not been significant in more than four decades, but many believe that is about to change.

The last half of the 20th century saw notable change in almost every arena of life. This was particularly true among the industrialized nations of the world. The development of the personal computer and the World Wide Web forever changed the nature of how we process information. The world became connected beyond anything previously conceived. For the first time in history, people began to think on a global scale. Things that were happening on the far side of the world were being observed electronically in our living rooms. We could communicate directly and almost instantaneously with practically anyone, anywhere.

Many of us were unprepared for these innovative changes. This was particularly true of the church.

Even today, as this is being written, the majority of churches are far behind the technological curve. Many function without even having a computer available to accomplish the most rudimentary tasks. Many overseers, especially in smaller congregations, accomplish their administrative activities on personal computers that they personally own and operate. This generates a difficulty that is often unnoticed.

The world is changing faster than the church. In most instances, we are not even attempting to keep pace with the developments that surround us. As a result, most people, especially in the United States, view the church as irrelevant and outdated. They do not see the church engaged in a way that is meaningful and challenging. The proof can be found in the way a minority culture advances its agenda at the expense of the majority.

Current statistics suggest that as much as 60% of the American public belongs to a church or religious institution. If that majority were to seriously follow through on their stated commitments, the culture would begin to see a significant shift that is not currently being felt.

DISCUSSION QUESTIONS

✦ How does the contemporary church tend to differ from the first century church?

✦ What elements of the first century church should be restored and which should be passed over?

✦ What changes are Christians being challenged to make as the Church moves toward a more apostolic stance?

CHAPTER
3

THE CHAOTIC STATE OF THE INSTITUTIONAL CHURCH

So, where does that leave the American church? This is a general question, but it becomes much more specific when we apply it to our own locale and our own assembly. Are we bound by tradition? Does institution paralyze us? Are we unencumbered by denomination? Or, have we embraced forms and structures that prevent us from functioning in the most productive and effective way? We know that the nature of denominations is to become institutional structures. What we often refuse to accept is that independent, fundamentalist, Charismatic, and Pentecostal organizations do too. As a matter of fact, most church plants and developing house groups tend to institutionalize rather quickly. We simply replicate what we know and are comfortable with.

Institutions establish operational standards that become rigid, inflexible, and unyielding over time. Institutions become intransigent—they resist change. They develop rigid patterns of operation, generate highly selective points of entry and erect subtle barriers to outsiders. Church growth is usually limited to those who are similar in culture, perspective, and background. The church in America is in such a state that there has been little or no net growth over the past few decades. People come and people go, but the church appears to remain unchanged. Every thing seems to be as it was, and nothing provokes us to develop a more effective means of making disciples. Worst of all, there is colossal resistance to change.

> THE CHURCH IN AMERICA IS IN SUCH A STATE THAT THERE HAS BEEN LITTLE OR NO NET GROWTH OVER THE PAST FEW DECADES.

THE CHANGING CHURCH THROUGH HISTORY

Across the past seventeen hundred years or so, the church has changed a great deal. More specifically, the church has been changed by the innovations and inventions of men rather than by the clear direction of God. There is confusion and disarray, not unity and focus. The theological landscape is littered with the varying opinions of man regarding what the church should believe, how the church should function and who should lead. Christianity has been served a smorgasbord of theological, doctrinal and ecclesiastical options. We live in a time when it seems that everyone is doing what is right in their own eyes. Instead of banding together and becoming communities of love and relationship, churches huddle up in select groups with theological and behavioral similarities and traditional norms, particularly in America. They find fault with one another and compete for the dedicated followers of Jesus Christ, rather than create significant inroads into the domain of the doomed.

When Moses led the children of Israel out of Egypt, he led them toward a more productive and prosperous time. In Deuteronomy chapter twelve, God set before the people His procedure for possessing the land that was before them. He told them (through Moses) that when they entered into the land, they were to destroy the idols and the worship structures of the people in that land. He told them they would need to obey His commands and His ordinances. They were to wait for the Lord to show them where they were to worship and to not simply do what was right in their own eyes.[1] We could use such instructions again today. Christianity in America, more than most of us would like to admit, is a hodgepodge of individualists, doing what is right in our own eyes.

People attend their church of choice for reasons wholly disconnected from daily life and experience. If their sense of spiritual need is placated, they see little need to become more deeply engaged. They fall into the subtle trap of separating the sacred part of their lives from the secular part. Somehow, they believe these are at variance with one another. Worship is primarily relegated to times of corporate celebration, quiet private meditation, or times of personal or family devotions. All too often, people fail to appreciate that there can be no separation between faith and their daily walk.

THE TRANSFORMED LIFE IS YOURS

God created us as whole, complete, tri-partite beings— spirit, soul and body. We were created in His image. Through the fall of mankind the spiritual part of our existence was lost. It was removed from God's presence and glory. It was dead. God, however, was not content to leave us in death. He set a plan in motion that would return us to union with Him. That is the most amazing thing. God loved us so much that He refused to allow the broken union between Himself and His image bearers to remain detached.

When we receive the transforming life of Christ into our being, when we are born from above in the act of God's salvation, our spirit is made alive toward God. Our entire being is then subject to the promise and power of His presence.[2] Because of this transformation, we have been given the capacity to be in perfect union with God. Because of this, we have been made partakers of the Divine nature.[3]

Why then are we not reaching out more and more, focusing our energies on those who have never believed? Why is there such a lack of concern for the souls of men? Why are there so many believers but so few who seem to be disciples? These questions force us back to the Word of God to discover the answers that will direct us to change.

Few, if any churches deny the Great Commission as a matter of doctrine. After all, it is one of the commands (if not the primary command) of Christ. But do we take seriously the command to make disciples? And if we do, have we institutionalized that process until it becomes merely another program within the church? Unfortunately, that seems to be the case.

> # INSTITUTIONS
> ## INSTITUTIONALIZE.
> ## THAT IS THEIR NATURE.

Institutions institutionalize. That is their nature. It is not that people want to squeeze the life out of the church, it is simply that they have no other paradigm out of which to operate. Programs, curricula, projects—this is the stuff that church organizations often use to direct, establish, promote, and achieve their discipleship goals. And I am not suggesting that they are necessarily wrong. Programs within the functional structure of an organized church can be quite good. They help to maintain organizational order and project a church through its responsibilities of tending to the flock of God.

THE NEED FOR ORDER

Every church structure, from home cell group to mega-church, needs an organizational framework. That framework provides order, direction, and strength. The problem arises when these organizational frameworks are substituted for the Great Commission. Programs do not make disciples—people do. Neither do organizations make apostles. Apostles are developed in the crucible of discipleship. They are hammered out on the anvil of service. They are called from within the depths of their being by the Holy Spirit and positioned by the Lord Jesus Christ. Apostles are allocated a sphere of authority in proportion to their gifting, their skill, and their faithful response. They govern. They teach. They establish and extend the work of God. They see the larger picture and strategize ways to achieve the ends God has planted within their hearts. But at the bottom line, their primary ministry is to make disciple-makers. Apostles are the lead people in equipping the saints (disciples) to do the work of ministry (make disciples.)[4]

> **APOSTLES ARE DEVELOPED IN THE CRUCIBLE OF DISCIPLESHIP.**

The call to Christian ministry has long been viewed as something of a separation between men. Indeed, it is. However, the sense of separation between the world of faith and the secular, or non-religious world is not a Chris-

34

tian concept. It is a religious one. Yet, even among Christians, the ministry is set against the secular world in such a fashion that practically everyone embraces that separation. That is because people tend to think of Christianity as a religion. Our assertion is that it is not. Although Christianity is the name we attach to the expression of our faith, Christianity is much more than religion, and cannot be separated from the daily life struggle of humanity without serious consequences.

FINDING ORDER IN NATURE

We see order and authority structures manifested in almost every animal life form, from the queen dominated societies of ants and bees, to the alpha males that rule the carnivores and primates. These, of course, are governed by fang and claw, and woe to the ruler whose strength wanes or whose wounds prevail. Only among humans are there divided spheres of authority that influence life and prevail. Those spheres are family, civil government, labor, and religion. One might try to further explain or expand the scope of the social order, but these are the primary spheres we recognize.

Each of these spheres has a specific set of rules or standards by which they function. Those rules may vary from culture to culture, but the people within that culture will respond to the rules in accordance with the way those rules are enforced. Strict and harsh enforcement leads to severe repression. Careless and loose enforcement leads to chaos and anarchy. Neither is acceptable in an ordered society.

The balance between personal freedoms and social responsibility maintains order within society. This balance is repeated and maintained in every sphere of our lives. Wherever there is a need for responsible behavior, there is need for an authority structure. Wherever there is an authority structure, there will be a kind of tension that maintains the equilibrium of that order. In human culture, religion plays an important role in the social order, even when that order is dogmatically atheistic. Even strict adherence to non-belief in a supreme being requires a kind of religious zeal and enforcement against the human need for identity in the divine.

> **THE BALANCE BETWEEN PERSONAL FREEDOMS AND SOCIAL RESPONSIBILITY MAINTAINS ORDER WITHIN SOCIETY.**

Religion is one of the most powerful influences known to mankind. It is unique among humans. From the animistic rituals of the most primitive of peoples to the complex hierarchies of the major religions of the world, people sense and desire a

> **RELIGION IS ONE OF THE MOST POWERFUL INFLUENCES KNOWN TO MANKIND.**

connection with deity. As far as we know, no other order of the animal kingdom is religious. If, among the amazing variety of life forms on this planet (other than humankind), any is mentally conscious or emotionally mindful of God, that has yet to be discovered. Only humans are known to sense a need for God. And in that need, mankind responds to the authority of religious leaders, often to the abandonment or the ignoring of other spheres of authority.

Reverence for Holy Men

For this reason, society tends to separate its "holy men" from the rest of the culture. This is true whether one enters the priesthood, becomes a pagan shaman, an Islamic Imam, a Buddhist recluse or a Hindu monk. It is also true for those who enter the ministry of the Gospel.

Those who embrace the religious as a life calling are viewed differently than are other people. Religion creates an aura around them. People see them in a different light, as somehow closer to God, or whichever deity they serve. Expectations regarding their lives change. They become the confidants of those who need counsel, the mediators for those who need forgiveness, the guidance counselors of those who have lost their way, and the advisors to those who are seeking insight from beyond themselves.

In India, for instance, one sees people by the thousands line up to have mystical priests daub their foreheads with red paint and pronounce blessings and protection over their lives. These priests are considered the very highest order in a society constrained by a severe caste separation and religion replete with superstition and mystical obscurity.

In the Islamic world, countless millions invoke the mantra of their faith. In times of prayer dutifully called five times throughout the day, they repeat the same words seventeen times, reinforcing the dominance that their religious perspective has over their lives. We see the mullahs, the religious leaders, exercising control over every facet of their society. And where the religious leaders are not in control, there is relentless pressure to elevate them to control. This becomes ever more noticeable as the extreme elements of that society provoke terror and violence in the name of their religious convictions. Religion is an overwhelmingly powerful force.

Judaism holds a similar supremacy, particularly among the Orthodox. They hold an allegiance to their faith that governs all of life—work, marriage, study, politics, and faith. From dress to diet to daily habits, they studiously adhere to rabbinical ideologies, many times with little or no understanding of any reason for such behaviors. The traditions of their faith govern most, if not all, of daily life. The Law, conveyed in the Torah (that sacred and dominant inventory of rules and order) holds powerful sway over the lives of all. The rabbis, the trained and ordained teachers and interpreters of the Law, exercise considerable influence over the life and structure of community. Backed by rabbinical Law, the order of the faith has great power. Simply stated, religion controls much of people's lives.

Okay. That's enough examination of non-Christian expressions of faith—we have our own problems.

There is far too much confusion among Christians regarding their own faith. Our faith community follows this familiar pattern, even though we would like to think that ours is different. Depending upon the local church body or the denomination to which a person belongs, the control exercised over people's lives can be significant. The level of that control is directly connected to the faith a person has in the leaders who exercise authority in that sphere. In some cases, that control is quite large. In others, it seems almost non-existent. However, within the Christian perspective, we find something quite different from every other faith group.

THE CHRISTIAN DIFFERENCE

Unlike most religious systems, Christianity is foundationally based upon a relationship with Christ, not on rigid adherence to an inflexible set of dogmas. That is not to say Christianity is without rules, laws, traditions, and dogma. Christian doctrine is quite specific and inflexible. The fundamental truths of the Bible, widely interpreted and often carelessly applied, are actually well established and unambiguous. Biblical faith is explicit. Salvation is by faith in Jesus Christ and His shed blood alone. The nature of God is clearly defined. His moral imperatives are absolute. The difference is to be found in the nature of the relationship between God and mankind.

In every other religious system, mankind is searching for God, working in some fashion to appease the deity he worships. In these, the pathway to a higher state of life, whether heaven, nirvana, or simply a higher conscious-ness, is paved with adherence to rules, specific behaviors, ceremonial sacrifices, or other ritual experiences. Even in the more modern extensions of Eastern religions, the trail leading to "higher consciousness" is based, not on a rela-tionship with God, but on self-expression, self-realization and self-centered focus.

THE RELIGIOUS DISPOSITION OF CONTEMPORARY CHRISTIANITY

Christianity, particularly in the West, is made up of a confusing tangle of ideologies. Most claim superiority in perspective, revelation, understanding and/or appli-cation. Theological differences, doctrinal specifics, tra-ditional forms and long-standing dogmas foster a great deal of confusion about what one should believe. Many churches have established practices and rules that are much more religious than relational. And, regardless of whether the structure is conservative or liberal, liturgical or contemporary, evangelical, charismatic, hierarchical, or democratic, the separation between the clergy and the laity continues to be a significant part of the religious perspective of people.

Christian authority structures are often quite controlling, creating a kind of religious dominance. People typically acquiesce to such leadership, particularly in spiritual things.

When this occurs, it creates spiritual or religious bondage, not to God, but to those authoritarian leaders. Leaders can hide behind a cloak of spiritual superiority, promoting themselves rather than the work they are called to do. The human tendency to venerate religious leaders has been part and parcel of human dynamics throughout recorded history. Why? Why are preachers and other holy men and women beheld with such a sense of reverence and awe? In some cases, such deference borders on worship.

SACRED MOMENTS, SECULAR LIFE, AND THE ROLE OF HOLY MEN

People usually prefer their spiritual leaders to be on a higher plane. They expect them to be closer to God, more in tune with spiritual reality. People are inherently spiritual. They recognize that a significant part of life is experienced beyond our natural senses. Yet, few really cultivate that spiritual quality. Instead, they rely on their spiritual leaders to interpret the mind and will of God for them. They are comfortable with this separation. Unfortunately, this clergy/laity separation has served to weaken Christianity more than to strengthen it.

> **THE CLERGY/LAITY SEPARATION HAS SERVED TO WEAKEN CHRISTIANITY MORE THAN STRENGTHEN IT.**

On a broad scale, people tend to look to their spiritual leaders for counsel, forgiveness, family guidance, or advice—particularly in matters they regard to be spiritual. Few seek such input into matters they do not consider to be on a spiritual plane. They fall short of integrating a significant quality of spiritual life with God on their own. These folk simply compartmentalize their lives into the sacred and the secular. They tend to be quite responsive to spiritual leadership as it applies to their faith life. They are far less responsive in the other aspects of their lives.

Business is business. Play is play. Family is family. Faith is faith. Unless an insoluble crisis arises, the religious leader is left out of the loop more often than not. Still, the aura remains around the religious leader—the pastor, the priest or the minister. People tend to walk around them in conversation. They guard their behavior when a minister is present. They cease to use coarse language, or relate stories that would otherwise flow freely. They cease to be open in what they say.

They further assume that God extends harsher judgment when these "holy people" are present than at other times. An inherent assumption lingers that such individuals have more power with God than do others, that they have a greater connection, a loftier position—something that is unavailable to the common man. Not surprisingly, this aura is often fostered by those who fill such religious roles.

The power of religious leaders is maintained and protected through ritual and tradition. Such rituals and traditions are deeply ingrained in peoples' mindsets, creating an air of spirituality that appeases the inherent need for God that is a part of human nature.

People also want to be close to a "holy person" in times of crisis, loss, disaster, or death. They genuinely desire to recognize the spiritual during significant rites of passage as well—marriages, births of children, funerals, etc. Somehow, the very presence of a pastor or a priest provides comfort or encouragement. At times like this, crisis or a life passage, people are open to prayer or spiritual incantations. They genuinely seek the solace of God's presence. The fragile fabric of life is more patently obvious during such times. People tend to feel that God is brought closer when a "holy person" is near. Thus, at times like this people look to a spiritual leader for strength. But when things are going well and life is good, these same people do not want to be held to a moral or ethical line that they have not drawn for themselves.

In many instances there is a very human assumption that God is angry or harsh, perhaps even a bit mean-spirited. People are convinced that God wants to judge their behaviors—and judge harshly. They would rather not have to think about or feel the overshadowing presence of the Almighty except in times of need. For those times, the presence of a "holy person," the invocation of a religious ritual, or the adherence to an ecclesiastical tradition might just serve to appease God. Light a candle. Offer a prayer. Give an offering. Do something religious. Then, they are free to go on with life as usual.

THE SACRED, THE SECULAR, AND HOW GOD SEES MANKIND

God is not placated through rituals and traditions. He is not appeased through sacrifices and offerings. The wrath of God was exhausted through the death of His only begotten Son.[5] The message of the cross is far more than a message. It is a point of transference—a place where the sin of man was consigned to the Son of God and the anger of God was eternally appeased. No longer was mankind subject to the harsh penalty of death. If he will but turn to the redemptive Son and receive forgiveness, the wrath of God can be diverted. If he will simply receive the salvation that God has provided, he can live a wholly integrated life. His entire spirit, soul, and body can be joined to God in a delightful experience of love, fellowship, and ineffable union.

> GOD IS NOT PLACATED THROUGH RITUALS AND TRADITIONS.

The work of the cross ended God's wrath toward humanity's sinful nature. Atonement was fully and finally achieved. God provided the way for mankind to come into the place of concurrence with Himself. Jesus' death fulfilled the righteous need for sacrifices, for altars, and for religious incantations. Jesus fulfilled the uncompromising mandate of the law and all of the predictions of the prophets. His final cry, "it is finished,"[6] sounded the death knell of religion as an avenue to God.

His resurrection, His ascension into heaven, and the outpouring of the Holy Spirit changed religion forever. Men and women had been at enmity with God since the fall. But with the coming of the Holy Spirit, God invited them into intimate union with Himself. The very delight Adam and Eve had known in the Garden of Eden—to walk with God and to have personal and intimate communion with God, became more than a possibility. It became more than even a probability. It became a certainty to all who would receive Jesus. These people, God calls His children.[7] These, He accepts as His heirs—heirs of His Kingdom, heirs of His promise, heirs of His blessing, heirs of God, and joint heirs with Jesus Christ.[8]

DISCUSSION QUESTIONS

✦ In what ways are people made in the image of God, and in what ways has this characteristic been lost?

✦ Discuss the nature of the institutional church and how it differs from a New Testament pattern.

✦ Discuss the church's acceptance of the role of professional ministers as opposed to the New Testament context of saints who are equipped to do ministry.

✦ In what ways is contemporary Christianity comparable to other religious expressions and in what ways is it uniquely different?

CHAPTER
4

A CHURCH
WITHOUT APOSTLES

Not everyone agrees that the church is in disarray. In many ways the church looks quite healthy. Beautiful church buildings dot the landscape, steeples rise majestically, and colorful backlit signs beckon people to come to the houses of worship. Articulate ministers crowd the airways, proclaiming the Gospel and encouraging both the faithful and the unbeliever alike. People feel blessed. Money flows. Things look prosperous and successful. But all may not be as it seems.

In the United States, for example, we have seen little real church growth since the late 1950's. True, some churches are booming, overflowing with new people and expanding beyond measure. But many others are losing strength. Some of the old denominations are drying up so quickly that they must

> IN THE UNITED STATES, FOR EXAMPLE, WE HAVE SEEN LITTLE REAL CHURCH GROWTH SINCE THE LATE **1950's.**

either merge with other denominations or completely close down. The vast majority of churches remain well below the one hundred mark in membership and have seen no significant expansion within anyone's memory. This is something that causes deep concern in the hearts and minds of people who have a determination to see the Great Commission at work. This may well be the reason that God is restoring the apostolic to the body of Christ.

As was stated in the first chapter, numerical growth outside the U.S. is nothing short of phenomenal. In conjunction with that, since the turn of the century, a rising tide of apostolic fervor has been developing. Paralleling that worldwide growth is the rise of the apostolic. Those who are embracing the apostolic are experiencing a significant shift in every aspect of church expression. The church is changing, and these people are determined to change with it. More specifically, they are intent upon changing it themselves— changing it as they are led and empowered by the Holy Spirit.

> THE CHURCH IS CHANGING, AND THESE PEOPLE ARE DETERMINED TO CHANGE WITH IT.

Those changes are directed at restoring the core infrastructure, the spiritual gifts, and the philosophy of ministry by which the church functions. To do so, they have had to look at the past to see what has gone wrong. What occurred during the past centuries in order to leave the church with a divided house (clergy vs. laity) and a stagnant growth rate? I suppose there are numerous reasons. However, one stands out in stark relief against the rest, so obvious that it has been largely overlooked by the mainstream of Christianity. It is the loss of the apostolic.

For hundreds upon hundreds of years the apostolic has been missing. Apostles have not been accepted or even recognized. Apostolic government has not been incorporated. Apostolic perspectives have not been embraced, and apostolic people have gone undeveloped.

This is changing. A time of apostolic restoration is upon us, and we need to take seriously the challenge to embrace it. The western church in the 21st century is by and large, hidden from societal activity. It is cloistered behind its stained-glass character, protected by its religious forms, traditions, and makeup. It is quite visible, to be sure. But, the effectiveness of its influence within society is questionable—growing weaker and becoming irrelevant.

What changes have occurred within the church across the past two thousand years? What (and who) delivered such impact upon the whole that it moved away from its apostolic roots and became the confusing conglomerate of ideas and ideologies it is today? To fully comprehend what happened, an exhausting study of church history would be required. But, enough information is readily available and applicable to provide us with a reasonable understanding of the changes the church has experienced.

THE DEVELOPMENT OF THE EARLY CHURCH

We are confident that the form of ecclesiastical government that was best understood among early Christian leaders was that of the Jewish community. When the apostles needed to expand the governmental order, they quite naturally followed this familiar pattern. This was not a violation of the Spirit's leading. It was in keeping with how God had established the culture long before the time of Jesus. So, elders (Gk. *presbuteros*) were appointed.

Jewish cities and communities had elders. They were not necessarily religious leaders, but were the wise leaders of the community who provided insight and counsel in matters pertaining to almost everything. There was a long-standing tradition of elders among the people of Israel that was not dogmatically religious. However, ancient Israel was a theocratic society in which the Temple, the Priesthood, and the Levitical order played a huge role. No member of Jewish society would have been totally disengaged from religious life.

The appointment of elders (or overseers in the church) beginning with the appointment of the seven in Acts 6, was an obvious progression. The church needed leadership, and that leadership took on the roles of oversight. We can be confident that early church polity closely resembled that of its Jewish counterpart. However, the original apostles filled the leadership roles, rather than the priests or the rabbinical councils.

The earliest believers were Jews and maintained loyalty to the Jewish faith, but that was soon to change. The earliest portions of the book of Acts bear witness to the fact that the church followed the teachings of the apostolic band within that Jewish context. But time and persecution have a way of fostering change. The rapid dispersion of the church away from Jerusalem, and the integration of Gentiles into the stream of believers had a significant impact on how the church operated and where it was going.

> THE EARLIEST BELIEVERS WERE JEWS AND MAINTAINED LOYALTY TO THE JEWISH FAITH.

Within only a few years following the resurrection of Jesus, heretical teachings began to emerge. In fact, many of the Pauline epistles were written for the express purpose of defining doctrine, establishing leadership qualifications, and validating the roles of leadership. The first three centuries of church history are a bloody record of prejudice against and persecution of the church. The period was marked by the rise of numerous heresies and heretical teachings. Such teaching espoused everything from overt sensuality to the denial of Jesus' deity or humanity.

The passing of time also brought a distinct decline in the use of the term apostle with a commensurate rise in the use of the term bishop. Some of the first and second century leaders were identified as apostles. However, we can surmise that the vast number of writings that were emerging under the names of apostles caused a reaction to that terminology.

Hermits and "holy men" also had an impact on the church. Some early Christians chose to isolate themselves and live as ascetics. They, like many of the heretical writers and teachers, wrote a great deal. It is difficult for us, in the 21st century, to appreciate the climate that surrounded the early church. The church had little written material to define its theology or doctrine. The apostles did not immediately commence writing. A rapidly growing Christian community without specifically designed guidelines was highly vulnerable to heresy and misapplication.

CONSTANTINE AND THE
DEMISE OF THE APOSTOLIC

History and tradition record the demise of the original apostles, but little is recorded regarding their replacements. What is recorded is the rise of ecumenical councils to deal with the heresies. More significantly, however, was the sweeping reforms of the church that occurred under the rule of Constantine.

As Emperor of Rome, this man, almost single-handedly propelled the church out of being a truly apostolic community into being an institutional, formulated religion. By an Imperial edict in 312 A.D. Constantine legitimized Christianity. Suddenly, not only was it permissible to be a

Christian, it was impermissible not to be one. The church breathed a collective sigh of relief. After almost two centuries of being ostracized, persecuted and disenfranchised, the church was drawn into the main-stream of society and respectability.

> **AFTER ALMOST TWO CENTURIES OF BEING OSTRACIZED, PERSECUTED AND DISENFRANCHISED, THE CHURCH WAS DRAWN INTO THE MAIN-STREAM OF SOCIETY AND RESPECTABILITY.**

Almost immediately, Constantine set about to redesign Christian worship, government and leadership. He legitimized the ministry—defining church leadership as a separate and empowered priesthood. He also granted reparation of losses that had been incurred over the course of time. Men who had been banished to work in mines or as galley slaves were returned to their homes. Estates that had been confiscated were restored to their rightful owners. Across a period of about ten years, through a series of Imperial Proclamations, his actions completely repositioned how the Church would function within the state.

For the first time, Christians were allowed to become state officials, both military and civil. Christian clergy, priests, bishops, and overseers were exempted from municipal burdens, just as Pagan priests had been. Constantine facilitated the emancipation of Christian slaves, removing the legitimacy of slave ownership that had long been held by Romans and by Jews. In 321 A.D., Constantine delivered an edict making Sunday the official day of worship, to be celebrated by cessation of all work in public. This served to permanently replace the Sabbath within the church, and effectively alienated the Jews. Among other things, Constantine was really intent upon removing all Jewish influence from the church, and because of the acquiescence of the Christian population at the time, effectively did so.

Ultimately, when Constantine became ruler of the whole Roman Empire, these edicts were extended to the whole realm. The Roman world rapidly became a Christian state, but it was a far cry from the Christianity spread by the apostles and their immediate followers. Instead, an age of growing darkness fell across the church, marked by the most vicious, wicked and heart-rending departures from the Gospel one could imagine.

> **AFTER CONSTANTINE, AN AGE OF GROWING DARKNESS FELL ACROSS THE CHURCH.**

The priesthood became a hierarchy with ecclesiastical titles that were quite removed from the responsibility assignments once understood by the Christian community. Ritual and tradition rivaled (and eventually outpaced) Scripture as the standard of authority. The division between clergy and laity became as distinct in Christianity as it was in every other religion. The hierarchy of the church exercised vast power—both religiously and politically. Sadly, the western world slid gradually into a time of superstition, fear, and subservience to papal prerogatives that lasted for more than a thousand years.

Notably missing from the history and literature are substantial references to apostles, prophets and evangelists. Parish priests carried out pastoral roles and seminarians took on the role of teachers. But the energy and passion for the Kingdom of God found in the early church, for the most part, ceased. What arose was a passion for conformity to church order and rule. People came into the church either by being born into the church or brought in through a system of sacraments. The advance of the church's domain was accomplished more at the point of a sword than through a transforming experience

> **NOTABLY MISSING FROM THE HISTORY AND LITERATURE ARE SUBSTANTIAL REFERENCES TO APOSTLES, PROPHETS, AND EVANGELISTS.**

with the Savior. In the midst of it all a remnant of people who had a passion for God and a living experience with the Spirit remained.

A THOUSAND YEARS OF DARKNESS

Over time, the institutional church dominated the world (at least the world of Europe, Asia, and Africa) but not without conflict, controversy, or schism. Any student of world history is well versed in the atrocities and excesses that mar church history. Power struggles were not uncommon within the hierarchy of the church, and in 1054 AD the church experienced a great division. East and West separated, primarily over which bishop should be supreme, Rome or Constantinople. The division marked the rise of what is known as Orthodox Catholicism. The eastern cultures followed the Bishop of Constantinople while western civilization was drawn largely into the Roman stream. Their bishop reigned from a throne in Rome called the "Holy See" with the title of Pope—heir to the throne, and the apostolate of Peter.

Eventually, the western church wielded such power that it became known as the Holy Roman Empire. Kings and rulers rose and fell, often at the whim of the Pope. While the eastern church remained much more connected with ancient traditions and practices derived from the great ecumenical councils of history, the western church slid into a period known to history as the Dark Ages, A time when the light of true Christian experience flickered and dimmed to the brink of extinction.

FORGIVENESS FOR SALE—
PROVOKING A REVOLT

By the 16th century, the church had reached a pinnacle of influence in the world, but had lost touch with the humble beginnings of the first apostolic age. Great cathedrals had been built across Europe. Rome was the religious power base of the world. In 1452, Pope Nicolas V commissioned the construction of St. Peter's Basilica. It was to be the "Pope's church"—the seat of the Holy See. Construction began more than fifty years later in 1506 when Pope Julius II laid the initial foundation stone. However, it was Pope Leo X (1512-1521) who is credited with provoking the Protestant Reformation. The extravagance of his Papal Court, coupled with the enormous cost of St. Peter's left the church in financial disarray. This overwhelming need for financial capital was met with quite a unique plan. The church would sell something called "indulgences." This became especially popular in Germany.

Conceived primarily by a Dominican friar named Johann Tetzel, the scheme was to sell these indulgences to raise financial capital for the church. This became a fairly wide spread practice in medieval Europe. In Catholic theology, forgiveness for sin cannot be complete unless and until penance has been accomplished. Penance, therefore, is little more than the accomplishment of specified acts that demonstrate repentance for the sin. Once completed, the penitent is purged, the sin is forgiven and its consequences removed. Theoretically, purchasing an indulgence served to demonstrate, in advance, penance for sin. Realistically, purchase was more likely made because the purchaser realized he or she would eventually sin, or even specifically planned to do so, and the indulgence would invalidate or remove the consequences.

In practice this was a method for prearranging sin and removing the spiritual consequences that would have to be faced when those sins were eventually committed. This was, in essence, a "Get Out of Jail Free" card. All one had to do was simply pre-pay (with money) the penalty for sin, and forgiveness was guaranteed. As you might imagine, the practice generated copious amounts of cash for the church.

> INDULGENCES— A "GET OUT OF JAIL FREE" CARD.

However, this and other outrageous practices provoked a firestorm of response from numerous clerics and Christian leaders, many who became the early reformers. John Wycliffe, William Tyndale, and Martin Luther are all names we recognize, even if we know nothing of their history. They, and many others, were moved to resist the abuses and machinations of the church. For instance, Luther's theology challenged the very authority of the Pope. He held that the Bible is the sole source of religious authority and that all baptized Christians are a general priesthood—a radical departure from Catholic theology. This is also a most apostolic point of view.

Luther wrote numerous books and articles addressing the many problems within the church, causing the Pope no small amount of consternation.

All in all, the sale of indulgences was the most visible indiscretion of the church. It was such a serious problem that to Luther's way of thinking, it was the ultimate disgrace of the church. He responded with his now historic challenge.

On October 31, 1517, on the door of the Castle Church in Wittenberg, Germany, he posted a list of discrepancies within the church that he was intent on debating. These 95 Theses became the core challenge to the church that ultimately provoked a revolution. Contention between Luther and the Pope grew so great that in January of 1521, Luther was excommunicated. The history of this period is a fascinating story that every Christian should read. Much that we as evangelical believers hold to be true today was brought into sharp focus during this time.

> **MARTIN LUTHER'S 95 THESES BECAME THE CORE CHALLENGE TO THE CHURCH THAT ULTIMATELY PROVOKED A REVOLUTION.**

Of course, these changes did not happen overnight. Luther and most of the others had little or no desire to leave the church. They simply wanted to address what they saw to be inconsistencies and errors within it. Over the expanse of nearly two hundred years, these men (along with scores of others) were moved of God with such passion that a transformation occurred across much of the western world.

Today, we call that time the Protestant Reformation. These were the emerging years for many of the churches we know today as the denominational stalwarts— Baptists, Presbyterians, Mennonites and Lutherans to name a few. The Reformation was used by God to stir sweeping changes across the landscape of Christianity. This mighty move of God is firmly established as a part of the heritage of every Christian community outside of the Roman and the Orthodox Catholic churches. Most of us are called Protestants simply because our spiritual heritage is connected to this time. But, the reformation did not restore the apostolic as a known reality. That would come much later.

WINDS OF THE SPIRIT— WINDS OF CHANGE

As a matter of course, Christianity saw numerous significant moves of the Spirit and revival events over the next five hundred years. Early America experienced several sweeping revivals as the Holy Spirit empowered men like Jonathon Edwards, George Whitfield and the Wesley brothers. Powerful encounters with the Lord took place across the countryside, in open fields, in brush arbors, and even in church buildings as the message of God's redemptive grace poured across the land. England also experienced noteworthy revivals. In Wales and in the Hebrides Islands, powerful outpourings of God's Spirit were recorded.

By the beginning of the twentieth century, God was ready to release yet another wave of change on the world. In various places, without collaboration, people began to receive an outpouring of the Spirit not unlike the outpouring recorded in Acts chapter 2. The Pentecostal movement had begun. Thousands embraced this new and controversial experience, only to find rejection and disapproval from their institutional church homes. Their response was predictable—they withdrew.

> PEOPLE BEGAN TO RECEIVE AN OUTPOURING OF THE SPIRIT NOT UNLIKE THE OUTPOURING RECORDED IN ACTS CHAPTER 2.

They isolated themselves. They formed churches, and eventually they formed denominations of their own. They embraced rules of holiness, practiced their then controversial doctrines, and sequestered themselves away from the mainstream of Christianity. They considered themselves to be, and in fact they were, spiritual outcasts. But within a hundred years, what they had embraced swept the world and released another series of significant spiritual upheavals.

For Pentecostals and those with Pentecostal heritage, the Topeka revival in Kansas, the Azusa Street Mission in Los Angeles, California, and a tiny church gathering in western North Carolina (now memorialized as Fields of the Wood,) are historical landmarks easily recognized. For the remainder of the church, they are of little note. But, these were the cradles in which the Holy Spirit's restoration of power and presence was being released, much like the first Christian Pentecost.

During the early part of the twentieth century great healing revivals occurred. They gave rise to forward looking expressions of church life, like the Christian and Missionary Alliance. The Latter-Rain movement of the mid-1940's eventually followed the Azusa Street revival and the Healing Movement. Some notable names, familiar to most Charismatic and Pentecostal Christians, are connected with this period—William Branham, Oral Roberts, John G. Lake, Katheryn Khulman, and Aimee Semple McPherson are but a few. With stuttering steps, a cry for the development of a five-fold ministry began to be felt during this time. The stirrings of apostolic renewal were at hand, but failed to really develop. In seeking to restore a more biblical structure, they failed to establish an apostolic platform from which to function.

FIFTY YEARS OF RESTORATION— THE FIVE-FOLD RETURNS

Almost in parallel but with a significantly different emphasis, the early fifties gave rise to a young evangelist whose ministry redefined evangelism. In 1949, Billy Graham conducted his first major crusade. It was conducted in Los Angeles, California. There he had three large tents erected for a three-week event. Instead, the ensuing revival lasted for eight weeks and set a precedent for crusade evangelism that has lasted more than half a century. Significant evangelism marked the decade of the 1950's. Church rolls swelled and it was a vibrant time, especially for the American church.

In the mid-sixties, another wave of the Spirit was released. Beginning with an Episcopal priest on the west coast of America, the Charismatic Movement swept the nation like a giant storm. This time it touched the mainstream of Christendom. Mainline Protestants as well as spiritually hungry Catholics embraced the baptism in the Holy Spirit, speaking in tongues, healing, miracles, and

> THE CHARISMATIC MOVEMENT SWEPT THE NATION LIKE A GIANT STORM.

the overpowering flow of God's Spirit. America was swiftly caught up with this fervor as the "changing of the spiritual guard" swept through the church. Indeed, the world was moved.

The Charismatic revival surrounded the globe. Every continent was touched. The power of the Holy Spirit touched millions until Charismatic and Pentecostal Christianity outdistanced every other Christian movement in growth and participation. In the midst of this refreshing movement of God something very unusual and important happened.

Powerful teachers of the Word of God moved to the forefront among Christians. Great teaching ministries were generated, and the church experienced a ground swell of revelation and insight unlike anything previously known. Unfortunately, not all of this teaching effected a better church. Perhaps some of the revelation was premature. Perhaps it was improperly applied. Regardless of the reasons, the church remained disoriented and in many cases widely divided.

Prophetic voices also emerged—voices with strong revelation and powerful insight. It is fair to say that the church was not fully aware of the restoration process, particularly as we see it today. But God was systematically rekindling the fire of apostolic passion, and the church was headed for a new day. Men and women began to sense that God was calling them, setting them in place with apostolic authority, and releasing them into spheres of authority and ability beyond anything they had seen previously. The apostolic was returning.

"I WILL BUILD MY CHURCH"

The church survived. Without embracing apostles or prophets, it survived through seventeen or eighteen centuries. This is an unassailable testimony to the faithfulness of Jesus in keeping His promise. He said, "I will build my church." In spite of the efforts of men, or Satan, or demonic forces or the circumstances of history, the church stands. In many ways, it is the church triumphant. But in many ways it is broken.

> **In spite of the efforts of men, or Satan, or demonic forces or the circumstances of history, the church stands.**

We can do better. We have better tools, increased revelation, the ability to see the weaknesses and mistakes of the past, and an elevated passion. We can address the problems in an effective manner. We can have the influence. We can shatter the "stained glass" wall of tradition, religiosity, and separation.

Now is the time. Today, more than at any other time in history, the church is positioned to truly be a transforming factor in the world. But to do it, the church will have to endure a transition. It must allow the Holy Spirit to re-engineer its structure and redefine its purpose, so that we return to the power, the presence, and the potential of our New Testament forefathers.

DISCUSSION QUESTIONS

✦ In what ways do you see the church as different today than it was in the first century?

✦ What changes did Constantine effect that repositioned the church and changed the way it operated?

✦ What was the primary cause of the Protestant Reformation, and what historical event marked its beginning?

✦ Discuss the ways Pentecostalism and the rise of the Charismatic paved the way for a contemporary apostolic movement.

CHAPTER
5

FORMING THE APOSTOLIC COMMUNITY—THE REEMERGENCE OF THE APOSTOLIC

It is fair to say that throughout church history there have been men and women who functioned apostolically. However, it is equally fair to state that they did not recognize they could have been apostles. They did not embrace apostolic authority or responsibility, particularly in the ways we see it at the beginning of the 21st century. But they were reaching, and the reach was in our favor. They opened the door to the possibility of an active and recognizable, contemporary five-fold ministry. Their revelation stimulated ours, and today, a genuine restoration is taking place.

Sometime around the middle of the twentieth century, in parallel with the rise of evangelism sparked by men like Billy Graham, a new movement rose out of old Pentecostalism. A significant healing movement was also taking place, involving such notable leaders as Oral Roberts, Jack Coe, and William Branham. Interestingly, this movement began to see several things in a fresh way. Their perspective was that God was restoring the whole five-fold ministry structure to the church. Many of them began to question the widely popular eschatological viewpoint of a pre-tribulation rapture of the church. Instead, they saw the church as being victorious. They noted that the prophetic pronouncements in the New Testament had already been fulfilled. They saw the bride of Christ, the Church, being prepared for the coming of the Lord.

> **GOD WAS RESTORING THE WHOLE FIVE-FOLD MINISTRY STRUCTURE TO THE CHURCH.**

APOSTOLIC STUTTER STEPS

Not genuinely knowing what an apostle was or what an apostle did, they explored the Scriptures, trying to define their new found roles. Without contemporary role models and mentors, their development was more often by trial and error than anything else. They had to learn by revelation and observation. What worked? What did not work? Was this the revelation of God or simply wishful thinking? The rising tide of apostolic understanding in the beginning of the 21st century cannot be separated from this time half a century back. The founders of the movement may not have understood where this movement would go, but they were confident it would lead to a more victorious church.

It is all too easy to assume that every new thought is a revelation from God. Not true. What we receive must be tested. It must be proven to be true, to be applicable and effective. This revelation of contemporary apostles and prophets was new, untested, and easily missed or misapplied. But these were sincere and dedicated people. They were determined to follow God. To be honest, some of them made unfortunate and costly mistakes. Sometimes they misunderstood aspects of how biblical authority was to be applied. In some ways they missed the relational connection between leader and follower as well.

> **IT IS ALL TOO EASY TO ASSUME THAT EVERY NEW THOUGHT IS A REVELATION FROM GOD. NOT TRUE.**

In their determination to build biblical order, some of them set up hierarchical governments and legalistic structures. In the very extreme cases they created the very thing they most needed to shun, and the repercussions were severe. Many people were wounded by the controlling nature of such leadership and many simply refused to embrace the revelation that had sparked their response to God's leading. These pioneers of the apostolic made a valiant effort and thankfully, some of them survived.

Today, several of them are still around to enjoy the out-working of their vision, and to know the delight of having other apostles rise and take the standard forward. These valiant warriors of the faith learned by falling down—but they got up again. They endured the punishment of criticism, adjustment, and misunderstanding to reach for and embrace the revelation God had placed in their hearts. Their scars are mute witnesses of their tenacity and determination to embrace God's call. In the process, God restored the ministry of the apostle to the church.

But how did it all start in the first place? How were the early apostolic days of the church different from the contemporary apostolic community?

THE BEGINNING DAYS OF THE CHURCH

To understand the apostolic correctly, we need to go back in time to the opening days of church history. Fifty days after Jesus' resurrection, on the day we call Pentecost, the Christian community exploded into life.[1] The release of the Spirit provoked dynamic growth in the emerging church that quickly swept the world. At first the apostles met within the confines of the temple day by day. They taught the very lessons Jesus taught. They presented the message of the Kingdom of God and people believed. New believers were quickly baptized into the church and entered into the life-flow of the Christian community. These new believers went from house to house, enjoying fellowship, sharing in the memorial of communion that Jesus had instituted at Passover, and eating their meals together. Also, they prayed.[2] They communed with the Lord together seeking guidance, seeking comfort, and seeking strength. They knew persecution and suffering were coming because Jesus had warned them that it would.[3]

The agony of Jesus' passion—His trial, His scourging, His humiliation and His crucifixion, was still fresh in their minds. But the joy of His resurrection sustained their hope. So they prayed. They spoke to God, and they listened to the voice of the Spirit.

Their faith controlled their lives. It controlled their thinking. It controlled their relationships, their choices, and their daily walk. They remembered

> **THEIR FAITH CONTROLLED THEIR LIVES.**

how Jesus had healed the sick, so they healed the sick. They remembered that He had expelled demons, so they cast out demons. But mostly, they made disciples.

> **THEY MADE DISCIPLES.**

They taught, and prayed, and drew people to Jesus, and—they made disciples.

The church grew. It expanded so rapidly that, as was mentioned in Chapter two, problems emerged. The initial population of the church was almost totally Jewish, but not necessarily Judean. Earlier persecutions and times of captivity had produced centers of Jewish life across the known, inhabited world. These disbursed Jews often traveled to Jerusalem at times of religious feasts and festivals. They came to worship in the temple and to offer sacrifices, something they could never do where they lived. Sacrifice was not permitted unless it was done in the temple, and sacrifice was at the heart of the Jewish religion.

Some of these travelers, especially very devout Jews, stayed. They made the traditional homeland of the Hebrews their own. They settled in Jerusalem and delighted in being at the center of Jewish life and worship. But they were different. They had been raised in other cultures, had developed their life skills and perspectives in a way that was probably alien to a Jerusalem mindset. These Jews who came from the far reaches of the empire were more Greek in their culture than the locals.

Problems, Prejudices, and Pre-Conceived Ideas

On the day of Pentecost, when the church was launched, there were Jews from everywhere. They all heard the testimony of the wonderful works of God in their native tongues.[4] Like the Judean Jews, many of them also believed the teachings of the apostles and united with the rapidly growing church. Unfortunately, it appears that the prejudice against them did not entirely dissipate with their introduction to the Gospel. Why would we think they were different from us? Is it unreasonable for us to assume that they brought their prejudices and preconceived ideas with them? Probably not.

Embracing the message of salvation, being baptized and entered into the church does not make a person a disciple. This was as true in biblical times as it is today. We bring a lot of old baggage with us into our new life in Christ—baggage that must be unpacked and discarded. This is particularly true with regard to prejudices, preconceptions, and established mindsets that are in opposition to Kingdom principles.

Discipleship takes time. A disciple cannot be made in a single day. For that matter, it cannot be adequately accomplished in a week or a month. Making disciples was the business the apostles were about. Obviously, they found themselves spending too much time taking care of the organizational and logistic needs of the growing church, and not enough time training disciple-makers. It was at this point that the original disciple-makers, the apostles, expanded the authority structure and embraced the addition of other leaders to share responsibility.[5] Suddenly there were leaders who were not apostles. One would become an evangelist. Another would be the

> **DISCIPLESHIP TAKES TIME. A DISCIPLE CANNOT BE MADE IN A SINGLE DAY.**

> **THEY HAD A COMMISSION—TO MAKE DISCIPLES, AND THE CHURCH GREW.**

first Christian martyr. And we can surmise that they taught their disciples to make disciples. They could not be put off by problems. They had a commission—to make disciples, and the church grew.

Following the death of Stephen, persecution fell upon the church with a vengeance. The Christian community scattered before the rising persecution like sparks from a fire. Everywhere they went, they carried the message of the Kingdom and they made disciples. Their message changed people's lives and they established communities of Christian love in place after place.[6] As the church grew and spread, the need for defined leadership grew with it. People with specific giftedness settled into places of responsibility, and with added responsibility came authority.

RAPID EXPANSION— HOLY SPIRIT DYNAMIC

We cannot, nor should we minimize the work of the Holy Spirit in this expansion. Everywhere we look in the book of Acts we see the fingerprints of Holy Spirit. He was present in a dynamic way, releasing them to acts that fell beyond the scope of their expectations. It was tangible. It was effective. And it was personal. His power was in them. His boldness empowered them. His presence comforted them, nurtured them, and sustained them. When they encountered people from other cultures, with differing ethnic backgrounds, non-Jewish ideas and pagan religious commitments, they were given wisdom in speech, supernatural insight and profound courage.[7]

It is impossible to separate the growth of the early church from the dynamic of Holy Spirit's presence. We cannot disconnect His direction from the development of church government, the establishment of leadership positions, or the improvement of organizational structure. All were under the overshadowing influence of God's Spirit. The record of Scripture does not allow us to miss this point.

> **IT IS IMPOSSIBLE TO SEPARATE THE GROWTH OF THE EARLY CHURCH FROM THE DYNAMIC OF HOLY SPIRIT'S PRESENCE.**

As early as Acts chapter 15 we find a council of the apostolic leaders wrestling with doctrinal issues and similar disagreements.[8] We observe the beginnings of schism as those who wanted a strictly Jewish faith got at odds with those who wanted a universally inclusive faith. We find instructions to overseers in Acts 20 where Paul, who had taken a lead role in the emerging church at Ephesus, instructs them.[9] James obviously becomes the spokesperson for the apostolic council and the leading overseer (senior minister) at Jerusalem.

This pattern is equally as important in a contemporary apostolic community. We see the principle of an apostolic leader, a "set man or woman" as the overseer of a local church. Or, we see an identical pattern of someone being "set" over a territorial region or a group of churches. This is the nature of apostolic government.

> EVEN THOUGH A LEADER CLAIMS TO BE AN APOSTLE, WHEN THAT LEADER DOES NOT LEAD APOSTOLICALLY, THE CHURCH COMMUNITY WILL NOT BE APOSTOLIC.

An apostolic leader is established in his or her position of leadership. Around that leader is gathered a council of gifted and faithful leaders, full of the Holy Spirit and wisdom. Together, they are equipped to perceive the counsel of God and provide leadership for the people. That leader is charged with the role of authority and the burden of responsibility. He or she might be a pastor, a teacher, or a prophet. But he or she will lead apostolically, or else the church community will not be apostolic. Even though a leader claims to be an apostle, when that leader does not lead apostolically, the church community will not be apostolic.

APOSTOLIC GOVERNMENT IN THE EARLY CHURCH

Notice how this scenario unfolds in the development of the early church. We see followers. Then we see followers who become disciples. Next, we see disciples whom Jesus names to be apostles. Then we see Jesus pouring His life into those apostles so that they will be able to lead apostolically. Finally, we see the church launched with apostolic power.

The church was initiated without administrative officers. As the need arose, the offices of responsibility emerged. Overseers or bishops were appointed. Elders were named. Without fanfare, prophetic voices arose and specific disciples prophesied. Either they were New Testament prophets or it is reported that they prophesied. There is no specific moment in time when the New Testament indicates a new call to the prophetic. The prophetic has been part and parcel of God's communication to mankind since the earliest days of humanity. The same is true of the teaching ministry.

> **THE PROPHETIC HAS BEEN PART AND PARCEL OF GOD'S COMMUNICATION TO MANKIND SINCE THE EARLIEST DAYS OF HUMANITY.**

Furthermore, the roles of pastors (who are nurturing overseers) and evangelists (who basically proselytize) are deeply rooted in the faith of the ancient fathers. Only the apostolic was a new thing within the new order Jesus brought. He was, after all, the apostolic prototype. He is our eternal High Priest and the chief apostle sent from God.[10]

The "five-fold ministry" over which we make so much, is only mentioned in a non-descript way until Paul, in Ephesians 4 specifically identifies these positions of gifted responsibility, and in 1 Corinthians 12 gives them an order of priority.[11] This priority established an order that best suited the purpose of God for the church. It did then—it should now. Only with the passing of time and the expansion of the church do we see specific distinctions other than disciples and apostles. Thus, the emerging church was, more than anything else, an apostolic church. It was a band of called out individuals (Gk. *ecclesia*), who were then sent out (Gk. *apostolon*).

APOSTOLIC COMMITMENT AND APOSTOLIC AUTHORITY

Since we are using the word apostolic freely, it is important that we clearly understand the difference between apostolic commitment and the delegation of apostolic authority. These are two uniquely different concepts. Apostolic commitment is the uncompromising dedication of disciples who are sent to make other disciples. It is a defining Kingdom value. In that sense, every Christian who claims discipleship also claims to be apostolic, or should. There is no real separation between these two perceptions. A disciple is not fully a disciple until he or she is actively engaged in making a disciple. Furthermore, that discipleship cannot be effectively evaluated until that newly made disciple is also engaged in making a disciple.

> **A DISCIPLE IS NOT FULLY A DISCIPLE UNTIL HE OR SHE IS ACTIVELY ENGAGED IN MAKING A DISCIPLE.**

Apostolic commitment is not merely about being sent into the world with the message of Jesus' love and grace. It is also about being sent into the next generation as well. There is a trans-generational component in discipleship. Paul, more than any other New Testament figure, modeled this concept, especially with Timothy. God's covenant promises are extended to His people trans-generationally throughout the giving of the Law and the pronouncement of His blessings.[12] He expects His promises to be extended to our children's children.

This trans-generational factor may well be the only real justification we can offer for calling those who are not our children by birth, sons or daughters in the faith. We do this because we are extending the life of God in us beyond ourselves. If we are not extending this life of Jesus beyond ourselves, that very life will die out. Indeed, that is one of the great miracles of the church. Across twenty centuries, the church has continued in spite of its weaknesses, excesses, mistakes and failures. Jesus' promise that the gates of hell would be unable to prevail against it remains intact.[13] The message of Christ has not been lost.

HOW DIFFERENT THE CHURCH IS TODAY

The transformation of Christianity, from its primitive, vibrant, apostolic roots to its opulent, ritualistic, religious expressions has not been achieved through biblical revelation or expanded discipleship. It has happened because men willfully and forcefully imposed their opinions into the order at the expense of the pattern. The church Jesus established is utterly different from the one we see today. That church exploded into existence on the day of Pentecost, captivated the people it touched with dramatic life change, and quickly spread across the known world.

> THE CHURCH JESUS ESTABLISHED IS UTTERLY DIFFERENT FROM THE ONE WE SEE TODAY.

The church was, for the better part of three centuries, a thorn in the side of the Roman regime. It was anything but mainstream society. Then, the thorn was removed. Slowly, ever so slowly the church changed. Political positioning fostered some of the change. Doctrinal struggles also contributed to the shift. These changes did not occur in a single day or a year or even across a single century. But they did occur.

We realize that men engineered the changes, some in far greater ways than others. Some had great power and influence. Others merely acquiesced to the pressures placed upon them. Legitimization seemed preferable to persecution. Acceptance is always more attractive than being ostracized. Three centuries of difficult living surely set the stage for embracing the extended "olive branch" of peaceful acceptance and prosperity.

Surely the emperor Constantine has been (or one day will be) faced with some very difficult questions. Many of our ancient revered and honored heroes may face a similar fate. But what about you and me? What kinds of answers will we be able to deliver when we stand before the awesome Judge of the Universe? I, for one, want to be able to say, "I saw the pattern and embraced the challenge. I accepted the call to make disciple makers."

CHALLENGING TRADITIONAL TEACHING

Such a challenge demands that we understand what we are about and what we believe. As an apostolic Christian, you will find yourself being drawn to some very specific biblical ideas and concepts. These may challenge some of the thinking and teaching you have been subjected to in the past. Remember, contemporary apostolic life is quite new, and in many quarters, unacceptable.

A significant portion of the church community has been and is being taught and believes that apostles no longer exist. That is, perhaps with the exception of the Pope. Roman Catholics truly believe that the Pope is a direct successor to the apostolic mantle of Peter. But, in general, the belief follows this line—that the age of the apostles ceased with the death of the apostle John, and that the twelve men whom Jesus chose were the only apostles. (Remember, you must remove Judas Iscariot from the list. Then, add Matthias, and eventually, Paul). Little or no explanation is offered to account for other apostles mentioned in the New Testament.

> **A SIGNIFICANT PORTION OF THE CHURCH COMMUNITY BELIEVES THAT APOSTLES NO LONGER EXIST.**

Those who claim contemporary apostleship are asserted to be false and heretical. Their character is assaulted because no biblical support exists to validate their call. The belief that the apostolic ceased to exist is called the doctrine of cessation. It simply means that the gifts of the Spirit (the "*charismata*"), along with the offices of Apostle and Prophet, ceased to exist at the end of the so-called "apostolic age."

This viewpoint assumes that the gifts of the Holy Spirit and the apostolic order of the early church ceased to be of importance. The only biblical explanation offered is a supposition that 1 Corinthians 13:10 refers to these things. "But when that which is perfect has come, then that which is in part will be done away." The biblical canon, actually the New Testament canon, is for those distracters, "that which is perfect." But the apostolic was fading long before the New Testament was ratified. Disputes regarding which books would

> **IF THE FIRST CENTURY CHURCH REQUIRED THE FUNCTIONAL GIFTS OF THE SPIRIT AND THE OFFICES OF APOSTLE AND PROPHET, WHAT MAKES US THINK WE DO NOT?**

be included and which were unacceptable raged well into the fourth century A.D. So, if "that which is perfect" was indeed Scripture, just when could it have closed the apostolic age and forced the charismata into disuse? Question: If the first century church required the functional gifts of the Spirit and the offices of apostle and prophet, what makes us think we do not?

Those who presume a cessation of the gifts and/or apostles lean hard on an arbitrary definition of what an apostle's qualifications had to be. In Acts chapter 1, the eleven felt it necessary to replace Judas. After prayer, they cast lots to see whether one of two men would become the replacement apostle. Their conditions were that (1) he had to have been with them at the beginning, and (2) he had to have been an eyewitness of the resurrection.

THE WEAKNESS OF CESSATIONIST TEACHING

✦ THE ASSUMPTION: if you were not an eyewitness to the resurrected Lord, you could not be an apostle.

✦ THE PROBLEM: this eliminates Paul as an apostle.

✦ THE JUSTIFICATION: Paul saw the resurrected Lord in a vision on the Damascus road.

✦ THE WEAKNESS: testimony alone validates being an eyewitness to the resurrected Lord.

How do we know this to be true? We have Paul's personal testimony. Only that! Like the testimony of Mary to her virginity, it must be accepted as true by believing the record. No other evidence exists. But for every believer, her testimony and Isaiah's prophecy are sufficient. Why? Because, they are recorded in Scripture. But then, we have only your testimony, and mine... and those of countless other men and women who have been touched, transformed and called by God to be apostles.

Many people have had similar visions across the centuries. Did that make them apostles? Not likely. Neither Barnabus nor Silas is reported to have seen the risen Lord. Nor did Andronicus or Junia, Aquila or Priscilla. Neither did Timothy or Titus. All of these people are identified, and seem to function as apostles in the New Testament church.

What makes an apostle an apostle? Apostleship is given by Jesus as a gift to the body of Christ. He or she is recognized in that position by the body of Christ and functions in a way that extends the Kingdom of God effectively within his or her sphere of authority. Scripture states that following the ascension, which occurred forty days before Pentecost, Jesus gave gifts to men—apostles, prophets, evangelists, pastors and teachers.[14] If He gave these gifts *after* the ascension, how could that be limited to the twelve who were given the apostolic commission during the first year of his ministry, three years earlier?

> **APOSTLESHIP IS GIVEN BY JESUS AS A GIFT TO THE BODY OF CHRIST.**

Simply put, the doctrine of cessation is wrong, not the continuation of apostolic order. Apostolic order was undermined by men, not removed by God.

> **APOSTOLIC ORDER WAS UNDERMINED BY MEN, NOT REMOVED BY GOD.**

But before we consider the roles of apostles within the apostolic order, it is important that we understand what the apostolic order is about. We do this by taking a look at apostolic theology. It is important for you to understand the primary difference between apostolic Christianity and other streams of Christian experience. It is also important that as apostolic Christians, we refrain from seeing ourselves as being somehow superior to others. Our revelation is fresh, our enthusiasm profound. But every fresh move of God repositions the revelation of the former move in some fashion and those who hold to that revelation have difficulty embracing the new.

> EVERY FRESH MOVE OF GOD REPOSITIONS THE REVELATION OF THE FORMER MOVE IN SOME FASHION.

Our responsibility is to discover God's direction and purpose for us and pursue it with abandon. We are the generation that God has blessed with the restoration of apostolic fervor. Our delight is to be in the current move of God. But should He reveal more and move the church to yet another level, we must position ourselves in such a way that change will not leave us in the past. We can manage change only if we are prepared to change. We can embrace the future only if we are willing to understand what heretofore seemed obscure, difficult, or impossible. So, in the next chapter we will take a brief look at apostolic theology.

DISCUSSION QUESTIONS

✦ What does apostolic commitment mean to you?

✦ List several ways a separation between the clergy and the laity has an impact on the culture of the church today?

✦ Briefly define apostolic government and how it affects your walk with God.

✦ Identify at least three biblical apostles who were not a part of the original twelve.

WE ARE THE
GENERATION
THAT GOD
HAS BLESSED
WITH THE
RESTORATION
OF APOSTOLIC
FERVOR.

CHAPTER
6

APOSTOLIC
THEOLOGY

Since the rise of the Jesus Movement in the mid-1960s, the consensus among many Christians has been that theology holds very little importance. Nothing could be further from the truth. Theology is central to your whole walk with God. Why? Because your theology is what you truly believe about God and how that belief is applied in your daily living. Your theology defines your morality, your ethics, your values, and your principles.

> **YOUR THEOLOGY DEFINES YOUR MORALITY, YOUR ETHICS, YOUR VALUES, AND YOUR PRINCIPLES.**

Theology delineates what we preach and teach. It establishes our understanding of everything, from the beginnings of the universe (creation vs. evolution) to the end of the age (eschatology or the doctrine of last things). It defines our moral perspective (absolutism vs. relativism).

And it clarifies our relationship to God (personal, intimate union vs. mediated sacrificialism).

THE UNIVERSAL PRESENCE OF THEOLOGICAL THOUGHT

Not only is the Christian faith defined by theology, non-Christian religions are as well. Each has a means and method of characterizing deity and people's response to deity. Every sacrifice offered, every prayer chanted, every invocation of an incantation is a response to a theological perspective. Every human on the planet thinks about God at some time or other. Even atheists have a theological viewpoint that they use to defend their non-believing, humanistic point of view.

Make a brief pass through the library in any seminary or Bible college. It will reveal a staggering accumulation of theological titles and subjects. What the Apostle John wrote at the end of his Gospel was an understatement, "And there are also many other things that Jesus did, which if they were written one by one, I suppose that even the world itself could not contain the books that would be written" (John 21:25). Perhaps the world has not yet been filled with such books. It surely is not because men suffer from a shortage of opinions regarding God, His Son, His Spirit. and His relationship to men.

The problem is not that everyone has a theological perspective. It is that, after seven to ten thousand years of human history, there are so many streams and channels it is impossible to fully explore. Christian theology is like a mighty river, flowing across the landscape of human experience for thousands upon thousands of miles. Flowing into that river are hundreds of tributaries, feeder rivers, streams, creeks, and springs. Each stream carries an idea, a thought, a concept, or an insight. Each has validity—at least to the person who initiates it and to those who believe it. Obviously, not all theological concepts are beneficial to all people. But all people engage in theological thought.

> CHRISTIAN THEOLOGY IS LIKE A MIGHTY RIVER, FLOWING ACROSS THE LANDSCAPE OF HUMAN EXPERIENCE.

I've often heard it said that God created man in His own image, and man has tried to return the favor. Perhaps that best describes the confusing array of theological opinions we encounter. What do I believe, and how is that applied to my life? How does that affect me in practical ways? How does that affect my relationship with God, with others, and with myself?

Am I trying to convince you to embrace a particular stream of theology? Perhaps. More importantly, however, is that I want you to have a basic understanding of a theological perspective that runs through the contemporary apostolic movement. Since we are looking at our faith through an apostolic grid, that only makes sense.

This apostolic movement includes many people from many backgrounds. Their individual theologies may offer opposing views. Even while laying claim to an apostolic perspective, there can be wide differences regarding specific issues of doctrine and theology. No single person has been able to articulate a theology that encompasses the whole of the apostolic movement. By and large however, we agree at this level. We agree that the apostolic perspective is forthright, uncomplicated, and biblical. In finding agreement, we find the common ground on which we can build together.

PRAGMATISTS NOT THEORETICIANS

Apostolic theology, often called "dominion theology," is never far removed from the realities of life. Apostles and apostolic people are, after all, not theoreticians. They are pragmatic warriors against the principalities and powers of this age and the heavenly realms that surround it. They look to the historical roots of the faith to define the directives they have received and to derive the authorization they need. Furthermore, they know the real and challenging struggles that face both the church and the culture in which the church must operate. This forces them to be "dominionists" regardless of their more philosophical theological underpinnings.

> DOMINION IS DIRECTLY CONNECTED TO CREATION AND TO MANKIND'S PLACE WITHIN IT.

In theological terms, dominion is directly connected to creation and to mankind's place within it. We refer to this as the "Dominion Mandate". Along with the Great Commission, this is the core Scriptural foundation for this theological perspective.

26 Then God said, "Let Us make man in Our image, according to Our likeness; let them have dominion over the fish of the sea, over the birds of the air, and over the cattle, over all the earth and over every creeping thing that creeps on the earth."

27 So God created man in His own image; in the image of God He created him; male and female He created them.

28 Then God blessed them, and God said to them, "Be fruitful and multiply; fill the earth and subdue it; have dominion over the fish of the sea, over the birds of the air, and over every living thing that moves on the earth."

Genesis 1:26-28

(Emphasis Mine)

Twice the word dominion is used. It is the Hebrew word *radah*, which means to subjugate or control. But in a greater sense, it means to reign or govern—to exercise rule. From the earliest communications God had with mankind, mankind was given the responsibility to exercise a God-like governance over creation. This responsibility was in keeping with the nature of mankind at creation. He was benevolent and compassionate, and exercised selfless oversight. After all, mankind was created in the image of God. God's image contained the attributes of God's purity. Humans did not know evil. They were simply a creation of good—until they partook of the tree of the knowledge of good and evil. Thus, mankind's dominion was not a ruthless domineering of the creation. It was made in the likeness of the One Who created it all.

> DOMINION THEOLOGY BEGINS WITH AN UNWAVERING BELIEF IN CREATION BY GOD.

Notice that dominion theology begins with an unwavering belief in creation by God. If God did not create the heavens and the earth, then the supposition of mankind's being directed to exercise dominion is without merit. This may seem overly obvious, but it is only one of numerous beliefs that accompany a dominion posture. Not all of them may be as easily embraced. Laying hold of a theology of dominion may well generate an eventual acceptance of other, less obvious conclusions.

Dominion is only one of a variety of theological premises that we need to determine how we approach the outworking of our faith. People who agree on other theological issues may well disagree regarding apostolicity and the concept of dominion. But people who are truly apostolic must recognize the validity of dominion. In order to truly embrace an apostolic perspective and the dominion principle, a person will have to know the basics of dominion theology.

Here, in a thumbnail sketch, I offer only an elementary summary of this position. It could easily be expanded into a much broader explanation. However, this should be sufficient for my purposes. I trust you will, at the very least, be able to articulate the relevant points of dominion.

BASIC OVERVIEW OF DOMINION THEOLOGY

MANKIND IS CREATED IN THE IMAGE OF GOD

Genesis 1:26—The first theological assumption is that of creation. On this assumption hangs the authenticity, veracity, and validity of Scripture. It is unrealistic to try to defend the inspiration of Scripture apart from the premise that God is Creator. It is exciting to see the ever increasing volume of scientific evidence being uncovered that categorically repudiates the premise of evolution and the concept of natural selection.

Mankind is Commanded to Be Fruitful and Multiply

Genesis 1:28—God intended for mankind to reproduce. Reproduction is a natural occurrence within the creation. This is true for humans as well as for animals and plant life. The inorganic does not reproduce itself in kind. But, the next portion of the verse indicates that humanity's reproductive responsibility was far more important than mere physical reproduction. It reads. "replenish the earth and subdue it and take dominion over it." This, as much as anything, suggests that reproduction was focused on the generational continuation of a governing order. Should any portion of creation rise up to resist the direction humans were taking it, they were to subdue it. They were to command, demand, direct, and require those created things to submit to their rule and governance. In a perfectly created world this would seem unnecessary. Unnecessary, that is, until you remember that Satan and his fallen company were all parts of the creation.

Satan was cast down to earth after his thwarted rebellion against God to overthrow heaven. He appeared to man and woman in the garden to tempt and seduce them. Adam and Eve were charged with the responsibility to take dominion over every living thing. But they turned aside. Instead of obedience they opted for information—revelation of evil, because they already knew good, and only good. They embraced Satan's deception at the expense of experiencing God's loving dominion.

MANKIND'S FALL
REMOVES MAN'S DOMINION

Genesis 3—Adam and Eve's dominion was lost. Some believe that it was given to Satan, but that is doubtful. The sovereignty of God cannot be assailed. Many scholars believe that the oldest biblical document is the book of Job. It seems to record events far removed from the patriarchal period of the books of Moses and those that follow. In this ancient writing, one discovers that Satan is totally subject to the will and directives of God. He must respond to the voice of God and submit to the demands of the Almighty. Satan was disallowed from violating the directives he is given regarding Job. That clearly demonstrates a lack of dominion. In the book of Matthew, Satan challenged Jesus with a level of temptation that suggests his domination of the earth. Yet, he cannot dislocate Jesus' conviction of the sovereignty of God. Only God is to be served.

Satan's influence is deceiving. Although his power seems to be vast, he is not God. Neither is he on a level comparable with God. The inspired writers of the Old Testament held that viewpoint. They were utterly confident that the Almighty maintained dominion. Jesus was also fully convinced that dominion came from God—and God alone. Nowhere does the Bible validate that Satan has dominion over the earth. True, he is powerful. He is identified as the prince of the power of the air. But, he is not identified as a king. Neither is he identified as a god. He is only identified as the accuser of the brethren.

GOD NEVER RELINQUISHES DOMINION OVER ALL THINGS

Psalm 24:1—"The earth is the Lord's and the fullness thereof, the world and they that dwell therein"—*including Satan and all the hosts of darkness.* 1 Chronicles 29:11-12—"Yours, O LORD, is the greatness, The power and the glory, The victory and the majesty; *For all that is in heaven and in earth is Yours;* Yours is the kingdom, O LORD, And You are exalted as head over all. Both riches and honor come from You, And You reign over all. In Your hand is power and might; In Your hand it is to make great And to give strength to all" (*Emphasis mine*).

Dominion was not given to Satan, it was returned to God. He retained it until Jesus came and delivered it to the church. He held the keys to the kingdom until he could give them to the One (and the ones) who were prepared to receive them. That is dominion. Satan may attempt to dominate, but he remains under the authority and the power of the Almighty, even to this day.

BECAUSE OF MANKIND'S SIN THE GLORY OF GOD IS WITHDRAWN

Genesis 3—Glory, the manifested character and the tangible presence of God were withdrawn. These evidences of that glory were released only in piecemeal fashion to specific individuals until the outpouring of the Holy Ghost at Pentecost.

Adam's sin plunged the world and its systems into chaos. Romans 5:12—"By one man sin entered the world and death by sin." Death and decay, unknown before this moment, suddenly became a part of man's experience. In instantaneous concurrence with the fall, Adam and Eve (and by extension all of the earth) were engaged in the process of dying. But worse than the decay of physical life, union with God was lost. The life of mankind was separated from the Life Giver and Sustainer by sin. Moral decay set in. Emotional decay became a part of mankind's fallen state. Survival became his struggle. God's perfect creation was damaged. It's character was now flawed. The glory was diminished and the world was plunged into darkness.

THE FALL OF THE FIRST MAN AFFECTED ALL MEN

Romans 3:23—Thus Paul wrote, "All have sinned and fallen short of the glory of God." Because the created order was altered, the reproduced order was brought into being under that alteration.

GOD WITHHELD DOMINION UNTIL IT COULD BE ENTRUSTED TO ONE WHO COULD ACCOMPLISH IT

Galatians 4:3-6—"Even so we, when we were children, were in bondage under the elements of the world. *But when the fullness of the time had come, God sent forth His Son,* born of a woman, born under the law, to redeem those who were under the law, *that we might receive the adoption as sons.* And because you are sons, God has sent forth the Spirit of His Son into your hearts, crying out, 'Abba, Father!'" *(Emphasis mine).*

Jesus, the last Adam and the eternal new man, is the one who could and would reproduce a new breed of children. That new breed would be the redeemed community, brought forth through salvation and made to be heirs—partakers in the glory, the honor, and the power as children.

Believers are The Sons of God

John 1:12-13—"But as many as received Him, to them He gave the right to become children of God, to those who believe in His name: who were born, not of blood, nor of the will of the flesh, nor of the will of man, but of God."

The Glory of God is Restored

John 17—Jesus' prayer is for the glory to be returned to the church. This return of the presence and power is to fulfill the responsibility of Matthew 28:19-20, to make disciples of all nations (Gk. *ethnos*) and to exercise dominion over creation Genesis 1:26-28

GOD REESTABLISHES HIS INDWELLING PRESENCE BY SENDING THE HOLY SPIRIT

Acts 1:8—"But you shall receive power when the Holy Spirit has come upon you; and you shall be witnesses to Me in Jerusalem, and in all Judea and Samaria, and to the end of the earth." The redeemed community has unlimited access to the presence and power of God through the coming of the Holy Spirit. Ineffable union is now both possible and probable for those who will receive it. The believing community is restored to God as children by adoption.

Romans 8:15-17—"For you did not receive the spirit of bondage again to fear, but you received the Spirit of adoption by whom we cry out, "Abba, Father." The Spirit Himself bears witness with our spirit that *we are children of God, and if children, then heirs—heirs of God and joint heirs with Christ*, if indeed we suffer with Him, that we may also be glorified together" *(Emphasis mine).*

JESUS ACCEPTS ABSOLUTE AUTHORITY OVER ALL THINGS

Matthew 28:18—All authority is ascribed unto Jesus, both in heaven and in earth. He is supreme sovereign over all things. He rules as King of kings.

ISAIAH'S PROPHESY OF AN EVERLASTING KINGDOM IS FULFILLED.

Isaiah 9:6—"...the government shall be upon His shoulders and of the increase of His kingdom there will be no end." Mark 1:15—"The time is fulfilled, and the kingdom of God is at hand. Repent, and believe in the gospel."

JESUS ESTABLISHES HIS KINGDOM IN THE EARTH.

Luke 6:13—"And when it was day, He called His disciples to Himself; and from them He chose twelve whom He also named apostles." Jesus commissions twelve governmental ambassadors (apostles) whom He trains to do the work of extending dominion through the process of disciple making.

THE RESPONSIBILITY FOR DOMINION IN THE CREATION IS MANKIND'S

Psalm 115:16—"The heavens belong to God, but the earth is given to the sons of men." This statement is a categorical endorsement of the dominion perspective. Redeemed mankind is to manage the earth and its resources from heaven's point of view. To do this, mankind must have the presence and power of the Holy Spirit and must operate within the boundaries of divinely delegated authority.

AUTHORITY IN THE CHURCH (THE BODY OF CHRIST) IS DELEGATED, NOT ASSUMED.

1 Corinthians 12:28—"And God has appointed these in the church: **first apostles**, second prophets, third teachers, after that miracles, then gifts of healings, helps, administrations, varieties of tongues" (*Emphasis mine*).

Two mandates are superimposed over the whole of apostolic responsibility. One is dynamic (Gk. *dunamis*), which is the ability or enablement to proclaim and make disciples of every people group. The other is authority (Gk. *exousia*) which is the responsibility to infuse the kingdom into the culture, the climate, the moral structure, and the economics, as well as the spiritual wellbeing of mankind.

The first mandate is held with a view toward the spiritual—the relationship between God and mankind. We call this evangelism. The other mandate is held with a view toward the physical—the relationships between people and collectively between mankind and God. The physical also includes the way mankind relates to the environment, the society, the culture, and the workplace.

THEOLOGY BEYOND THE APOSTOLIC

Christian theology offers a vast assortment of concepts and ideas. Even a casual glance at the field becomes daunting to the most avid student. Dozens upon dozens of theological configurations create a patchwork of Christian thinking and conviction. Each defends a particular point of view or peculiarity of thought. Some try to defend non-biblical perspectives. Others cling to traditionalist ideas that have long since been passed over by the main stream of the faith.

Christian seminaries often divide theology into four groupings—exegetical, historical, systematic, and practical. I will not attempt to define each of these. However, if we were to categorize apostolic theology, it would be a combination of historical theology and practical theology. We reach back into the beginnings of the church to discover the form and structure of our faith, and we look to the functionality of our relationship with God to discover how that faith should be applied in the 21st century.

This is our system—that is, this is the system I use. Many of my contemporaries do also. In so doing, we establish and promote our beliefs about redemption, about Jesus and His atoning work, about charismatic gifts, and about a host of other things that make us who we are as believers.

> ONCE OUR THEOLOGY HAS BEEN ESTABLISHED, IT NO LONGER CAPTIVATES OUR CONSCIOUSNESS.

Once established, however, our theology no longer occupies the foreground of our consciousness. It resides in the background, shaping our responses to life circumstances, stimulating our disciplines, anchoring our morality, and stabilizing our ethics. Our theology often instinctively corrals us into comfortable groupings of like-minded people. Our theology protects us and keeps us alert to things we do not believe. It also keeps us sensitive to what we need to learn. It is always evolving, growing, and expanding. It embraces our experiences and our learning. And if it is strong, it gives us strength. It fortifies our confidence in our God and strengthens our resolve to walk worthy of Him.

Your theology is not limited to this dominion structure. It is much broader than this, even if you are unaware of that fact. However, as an apostolic Christian, nothing you believe, nothing you proclaim, and nothing in your walk with God will be unaffected by His mandate to walk in dominion and make disciples.

DISCUSSION QUESTIONS

✦ What is the Dominion Mandate?

✦ What is the Great Commission?

✦ How do these affect your perspective of your daily Christian experience?

✦ Discuss Apostolic Theology and how this perspective influences other aspects of your basic Christian beliefs.

CHAPTER
7

THE CHURCH, THE KINGDOM, APOSTLES, AND APOSTOLIC LEADERSHIP

Apostolic authority is a governmental concept. Apostolic theology is established on that premise. God instructed Adam and Eve, and by extension all mankind, to function as the overseers of creation. They would rule over the fowls of the air, the fish of the seas, and the beasts of the earth. And they would have the ability to use plant life of the earth as food for their lives.

The fall of man did not eradicate the mandate—it complicated it. Before the fall, mankind's work produced predictable results. After the fall, the earth fell under a curse. Plants that had once been identified as desirable and edible (because they bore seed) became inedible, undesirable, and even toxic. People now had to discern what they could or could not eat, quite possibly by suffering adverse physical reactions to their attempts. Creatures once docile became ferocious. Most likely some of them even became venomous. Were they so before the fall? We do not know, but venomous or not, they were still responsive to the direction and dominion of mankind.

Today, we are confident that the mandate of dominion is still in force. We believe that God has established an eternal government under the rule and reign of Jesus Christ. He came, announcing the presence of the Kingdom of God, and accepting His position as King of kings and Lord of lords. Isaiah prophesied of Him, Isaiah 9:6-7;

> *"For unto us a Child is born, Unto us a Son is given; And the government will be upon His shoulder. And His name will be called Wonderful, Counselor, Mighty God, Everlasting Father, Prince of Peace. Of the increase of His government and peace There will be no end, Upon the throne of David and over His kingdom, To order it and establish it with judgment and justice From that time forward, even forever. The zeal of the Lord of hosts will perform this."*

It was this government that Jesus came to establish and rule. It is the government of the Kingdom of God—established by God's direction, accomplished in God's timing.

Jesus announced the coming of the Kingdom long before He instituted the church in the New Testament. Now notice, the church is not the Kingdom and the Kingdom is not the church. However, the church is in the Kingdom and the Kingdom is in the church. The church was designed to be the visible, tangible expression of the Kingdom within the confines of culture and society. The Kingdom is nothing less than the reign of God over all things, both visible and invisible, past, present, and future.

> **THE CHURCH IS NOT THE KINGDOM AND THE KINGDOM IS NOT THE CHURCH.**

ADDRESSING CONFUSION REGARDING THE CHURCH

One of the common mistakes we make as Christians is to confuse the concept of church with the concept of Kingdom. When we do this, our response is to confine Kingdom activity and perspective to the infrastructure and activities of the church. With the innovation of dedicated facilities, the church was able to visibly demonstrate its presence wherever it existed. But that demonstration soon took on the persona of the church and, for the vast majority of people, became the church. Inextricably linked to the people who gathered there, the church became largely isolated to the confines of activity and relationship within a building.

The separation between clergy and laity, between pulpit and pew, was a distortion that grew out of Constantine's modifications of the church's function and worship structure. It was made worse by the church's acceptance of that separation. By compartmentalizing people's thinking into sacred and secular, a specialized order of men was created whose sole responsibility was to manage the spiritual side of life.

THE CHURCH IS THE COMPANY OF CALLED OUT ONES WHO HAVE DECLARED THEIR ALLEGIANCE TO JESUS CHRIST.

The church is the body of Christ, nothing more, nothing less. The biblical word for church is the Greek word *ecclesia* which means "the called out, or a calling out." Thus, the church is the company of called out ones who have declared their allegiance to Jesus Christ and His Kingdom. The church is to gather periodically for collective worship, training, and encouragement. That period may be weekly. It is often conducted on Sundays. It could just as righteously be accomplished on a different schedule.

The contemporary church gives the impression that this gathering together is the primary responsibility for Christians. Faithful attendance to corporate gatherings for worship, coupled with overt moral excellence is, by and large, the rudimentary expectation in most church organizations. Add to that, faithful giving to support the programs and initiatives, finance the care of staff and facilities, and send a portion to other ministry focal points—that is supposed to be the church. But is it, or does that merely define a congregation? And if it is the church, is that the way the Kingdom operates?

THE UNIVERSAL MAKEUP OF THE KINGDOM

The Kingdom is quite different from the church in many ways. All of the values and intensity of the church exist within the Kingdom, to be sure. But the Kingdom extends far beyond the boundaries of congregational infrastructure. The Kingdom touches every area of life, every structure of society. The concept of dominion is directed at empowering and energizing a transforming force in all of the areas of culture and society, even though it may be invisible.

The Kingdom manifests as the Christian community becomes the "salt and light" of transformation wherever individual Christians find themselves. Work, play, business, education, governmental responsibility—everything is influenced by a truly Kingdom community. It is, in the purest sense, church. But as church, it engages all that surrounds it with "righteousness, peace and joy in the Holy Ghost."[1]

To extend, maintain, and preserve this Kingdom in the earth, Jesus named apostles. After Jesus returned to the Father, these apostles established the church. They governed the activities of the church. They obviously prepared others to carry on the work of guiding the church.

Eventually Jesus named others to be apostles, not by meeting them on a mountain, but by the indwelling power of the Holy Spirit. Called by God, they were first qualified in character and then gifted in ministry. They were established in responsibility and recognized in their positions of authority. They did not make the leap from new believer to apostle instantaneously. What makes us think that would happen today?

RECOGNIZING AND AFFIRMING APOSTLES TODAY

Paul warned Timothy, his apostolic protégé, neither to lay hands on someone too quickly,[2] nor to ordain a novice.[3] Contemporary apostles must be careful to exercise commensurate care. The rise of the apostolic in the 21st century has given rise to an outpouring of ill-prepared, unqualified, zealous neophytes who reach for position long before they have endured the crucible of preparation.

A person does not have to be a hardened old veteran of denominational wars to become an apostle. Far from it. Youth is an attribute. But unbridled youth can prove to be a detriment to the expansion of Kingdom rather than an asset.

The original apostles were most probably men in their mid to late twenties when they were called by Jesus. However, they were not immediately released into positions of primary leadership. They went through an intensive period of hands on, in-your-face development. Their

> **THE FIRST APOSTLES WERE SCHOOLED IN THE MIRACULOUS, DISCIPLINED IN DELIVERANCE, AND DEMONSTRABLY SHOWN HOW TO LEAD.**

training was not some three-year Bible college course in traditional church polity and escapist eschatology. They were schooled in the miraculous, disciplined in deliverance, and demonstrably shown how to lead. Jesus was their teacher—personally.

Would you desire to sit at the Master's feet and hear the words of life from His own lips? Of course, but that is not our lot. Rather, we are to integrate the message into our lives in such a way that our actions match those of the early apostles. Our zeal must be real. Our passion must burn with the intensity of vision and victory. We must rightly discern the words of Scripture and fearlessly stand in the places of authority we have been commissioned to fill.

A major problem with youth is that the young act as though they will never grow old. Like the ambitious son in the parable of the prodigal, they want it all right now.

Not all youth are like this, mind you, but far too many of our emerging and budding apostolic leaders are plagued with an impatience that can only dissipate as they mature. Older, wiser apostles and apostolic leaders need to rein them in so that they will not be spoiled for the future. Proper training and sensible coaching are required. Inadequate training and unbridled zeal often lead to riotous living and the squandering of resources.

Young or inexperienced, zealous apostles and apostolic leaders must exercise care in trying to have a larger sphere of authority than they can legitimately handle. God has good reason for allowing a cranky old elder or deacon to be in their lives. Like an old, wise ram who gruffly keeps the flock in line, these folk have seen more, heard more, lived through more, and overcome more than can be imagined. Never holding apostolic authority themselves, they stand as counsel to the king, so to speak. Scripture rightly commends us to honor those with the hoary heads of wisdom.[4]

However, there are many "wannabe" apostolic aspirants, both young and old. Seduced by the lure of greater notoriety, they are desirous to be at the pinnacle of the ecclesiastical ladder. A new title looks like a tasty plum on the "ministry tree." Some are tired of being less than successful in what they see to be lesser responsibili-

> **IF AMBITION DRIVES THE DESIRE, THE RESULT WILL BE CHAOS.**

ties. Others just want to be "the boss." If ambition drives the desire, the result will be chaos.

RECOGNIZING THE CALL AND ANOINTING OF APOSTLES

Most people will never be apostles, nor should they be. The ministry role of an apostle is a highly specialized task that demands something far beyond the will and whim of most people. Furthermore, it is not a ministry goal to be pursued. Apostles are often a target for misunderstanding, criticism, false or meaningless accusations, and a host of other challenges. Becoming an apostle makes a person an instantaneous target for elevated satanic attack. Spiritual warfare becomes a way of life. The demands are intense. This elevated responsibility requires a life lived far above the level of being common or trite. Rest assured, God is very selective concerning who He gives to the body of Christ as an apostle.

No person has the responsibility or the right to appoint himself or herself, or anyone else to be an apostle. Christ Jesus, not a board or an electorate, appoints apostles. He did in the beginning. He does now. The Holy Spirit, present in full measure in the man Christ Jesus, is now present within the lives of His many-mem-

> **CHRIST JESUS, NOT A BOARD OR AN ELECTORATE, APPOINTS APOSTLES.**

bered body, the church. When He calls an individual to be an apostle a process begins.

Almost immediately, that person experiences a "de facto" elevation in anointing and authority. There is no formal announcement, ceremony, or ritual. There is simply a mutually experienced expansion of opportunity and function. The church, by recognizing that anointing and responding to that elevated influence, begins to validate what the Spirit is doing. The individual's sphere of influence expands. His or her wisdom is recognized and the demands of apostolic function begin to emerge.

Although he or she may know deep within that the Lord has called them and appointed them to be apostles, it is not their responsibility to announce it. Recognition of a true apostle will come in due season. Other apostles are looking for these newly called brothers and sisters. These older apostles are committed to the raising up of the next generation. They deeply desire to see them adequately trained and properly commissioned. But, they are not in a hurry, because they know the pitfalls. They have seen the destruction that has occurred when someone is not prepared to function as an apostle, or worse, is not really an apostle at all.

How long does it take? What is the training cycle from being called to being commissioned? No one knows for sure, except perhaps Jesus. It took Him three full years of intense discipleship to prepare the first twelve, and one of them washed out. We would do well to remember that. The Apostle Paul, the most highly educated theologian of his day, spent three years in exile in preparation.[5] It is all too easy for us to project a quality onto the lives of that first apostolic company different from our own. They had more... what? Charisma? Power? Knowledge? Passion?

Assessing The Difference

What did they have that is unavailable to every believer today, other than to have been personally trained by Jesus? And that being said, remember that there is no record that they had the Holy Spirit like you and I have available. In fact, they were not filled with the Holy Spirit until after the crucifixion,[6] and they were not empowered by the Holy Spirit until Pentecost, forty days after Jesus had ascended into Heaven.

Do not believe that the first apostles had more and better tools. They didn't. Do not believe they had revelation that is unavailable to you. They didn't. And do not believe that they had power beyond that which God is capable of imparting to you. They did not. Moreover, you have treasures and tools the original apostles never had.

> **You have treasures and tools the original apostles never had.**

You have the completed canon of Scripture. You have their wisdom, their insight and God's chosen, objective revelation contained in a volume of such remarkable value it remains the most important, best selling, and most widely read document in the whole world.

APOSTLE IS NOT A VERB

One would be hard pressed to believe that, having been called to the apostleship by Jesus, any individual would not have to experience a time of intense spiritual training. He or she should have to demonstrate a significant level of power and a notable, natural rise in authority. That person would also need to experience the recognition of the apostolic call by other apostles.

The word apostle has no active verb form. All the other gifts do. You can exercise the word of wisdom. You can discern a spirit. You can speak in another tongue and interpret those tongues. You can teach. You can prophesy. You can pastor, or nurture the flock and you can evangelize. But you cannot "apostle." The verb form of apostle is passive. In other words, an individual can be acted upon but not self-determined. An individual can be "apostled," that is, be sent. If "apostled" was a word, that is what it would mean. It comes from the Greek word, *apostello*, which means a specific act of sending with a mission. But no one can "apostle" himself or herself. No one is given license to "self-send" as it were. Apostles are only sent by Jesus.

The gift of apostle is not uniquely a gift. It is an amalgamation—a mixture of all the things God has placed within an individual to become the leader they are. Many apostles are also prophets or teachers. Many are pastors or administrators who have become particularly savvy at directing church affairs. Others are combinations of several functional capacities working collectively within a person's life. All apostles have a broad range of activated spiritual gifts working within their lives. But they do not "apostle." They lead.

THE FUNCTIONAL RESPONSIBILITIES OF APOSTLES

Each apostle is as unique as his or her personality, coupled with the mixture of gifts, experiences, and responsibilities they carry. To try to specifically define all that an individual apostle does (or is responsible to do) is beyond the scope of any manuscript. Try to pin it down to a single thing or a punch list of responsibilities, and something will break the pattern. You might try to define the specific territory of an apostle and limit him or her to that alone. But be careful. God can and may quickly expand his or her territory while you are not watching.

> APOSTLES ARE REQUIRED TO EXERCISE AUTHORITY BY DIRECTING THE LIFE FLOW OF THE CHRISTIAN COMMUNITY.

Apostles are required to exercise authority by directing the life flow of the Christian community. This is a process more of leadership than of command. They exercise authority by relationship and influence far more than by control. Theirs is a responsibility to serve, not to be served. They are not to lord over people.[7] While they are, in many instances, the rulers (overseers) of the church, they are to exercise their responsibility in the manner in which Jesus exercised His. They are servants as well as leaders.

This is true of all of the five-fold ministries listed in Ephesians 4—apostles, prophets, evangelists, pastors, and teachers. These are given the task of equipping the saints (that is the Kingdom community) to do the work of ministry. That community, in turn, is to manifest the Kingdom of God within the culture and the society to such a degree that heaven's influence is felt in the earth. They are to function within the capacity of that particular field in which Jesus has placed them.

One of the common mistakes people make is to assume that an individual has been given a "five-fold" gift. Every individual who occupies any of the five-fold offices or functional ministries is far more than what the title implies. Unlike the charismata of 1 Corinthians 12, or the gifts listed in Romans 12, the five-fold gifts are not distributed to individuals. They are given to men—plural. It is consistent with good exegesis to realize that this giving is not to the individuals who function as five-fold leaders. Rather, these leaders are the gifts. The composite of their multifaceted gifting establishes their unique capacity to fulfill their various assignments within their own particular spheres of influence.

THE UNIQUE QUALITY OF A GIFT MIX

No two five-fold ministers are alike. They are each unique, having both an individual and a precise mixture of gifts. They are specifically prepared to achieve the ends to which God has sent them. The various charismatic gifting they carry—healing, miracles, tongues, words of wisdom, etc., all have identifiable and similar qualities. Healing is measured by the fact that people are healed. Tongues is a common expression that bears remarkable similarity from one speaker to another—speaking a language they never learned. Prophecy often carries a remarkable similarity from one speaker to the next. The one who prophesies speaks as the voice of God in the moment, offering edification, exhortation and/or encouragement.

An apostle cannot be "pigeon-holed," that is, there is no specific job description that fits every apostle. A prophet cannot be constrained to a defined structure. The five-fold is not given for command, though at times command is required. It is given for function, so that the church (the body of Christ) can be equipped to function as Kingdom in every situation of life. To reduce any of the five-fold functions to a confined definition, or to merely establish a particular term as a position or title is to do violence to their function. True,

> **THE FIVE-FOLD IS NOT GIVEN FOR COMMAND—**
>
> **IT IS GIVEN FOR FUNCTION.**

an apostle is a titled person, but the title is meaningless unless the function is established. A prophet, upon recognition and acceptance by the body, is titled. He or she is not a prophet because of the title, however. Neither is he or she a prophet because he or she prophesies. Every member of the body is given permission to prophesy.[8] Simply put, a true prophet is a gift, given to the body by Jesus. That prophet does not function by convention, cannot be duplicated and is not limited to man-made boundaries.

> **A TITLE IS MEANINGLESS UNLESS THE FUNCTION IS ESTABLISHED.**

LEADERSHIP—THE BASIS OF APOSTOLIC AUTHORITY

As the church presses more deeply into its apostolic stance, an understanding of apostolic leadership will become more and more necessary. Basically, apostolic leadership can be defined as every leadership responsibility within the church. The requirement will be the same, to operate under apostolic authority and prophetic insight. We will discuss this further in the next chapter. However, every office, every ministry function, every person who is responsible for the training and development of any other Christian person at any level, is involved in apostolic leadership. This includes elders, deacons, administrators, Sunday School teachers, musicians, worship personnel, intercessors, counselors, instructors, group leaders, ushers, and every other member of the church infrastructure. But apostolic leadership goes even beyond that.

From the church, it extends to the workplace, the culture, and the society. The church must continue its influence beyond the confines of the building, its environs, and its place in the community. The influence of Kingdom must be felt in business decisions, in educational presentations, in the development of the arts, in government, and in the media. Wherever the body of Christ is manifested,

> **WHEREVER THE BODY OF CHRIST IS MANIFESTED, THE PRESENCE OF THE KINGDOM IS AVAILABLE TO EXERT INFLUENCE.**

the presence of the Kingdom is available to exert influence. When that influence is exercised, good things begin to happen. When it is not, the power of the prevailing culture dominates the moment.

Apostolic leadership should consistently recognize and promote the fact that we, the whole body, are "apostled," so to speak. (*So, I created a verb form for apostle. I trust my readers will get the meaning.*) That is, we are sent out into the world to be a living expression of the Kingdom within the context and confines of the culture that surrounds us. We are to be both salt and light.[9]

Certainly in every one of these expressions of the body of Christ, the church exists. The church contains them all, and collectively it is the means God has chosen to extend His Kingdom into the earth. He is building His church, even to this day, and none of us is sufficiently informed to unequivocally declare that the widely divergent Christian expressions are not a part of the church. Indeed, we should affirm that they are, at least most of them are. And if they are, we should also be aware that they are a part of the Kingdom of God.

DISCUSSION QUESTIONS

✦ Discuss both the differences and the similarities you see between the church and the Kingdom.

✦ What characteristics tend to identify and validate an apostle?

✦ What impact do the terms apostle, apostolic and "apostled" have on your thinking, your commitment, and your Christian experience?

✦ Discuss the importance of apostles experiencing a maturation process before having wide ranging responsibility.

THE GIFT OF
APOSTLE IS NOT
UNIQUELY A GIFT.

IT IS AN
AMALGAMATION—A
MIXTURE OF
ALL THE THINGS
GOD HAS PLACED
WITHIN AN
INDIVIDUAL
TO BECOME THE
LEADER THEY ARE.

IDENTIFYING THE APOSTLES— DEFINING THE CHURCH

Far too many people look at the church as if it were the little white building on the corner of "Somewhere and Vine." Usually, this is what we mean when we think of the local church. It can be quite small, or it can be numbered in the multiplied thousands. It can be urban, suburban, community, or rural. It can be ethnically unmixed or culturally blended. It can be rich or poor, formal or informal. It can be highly diversified or dominated by a single family. It can be denominationally oriented or an expression of independence. It can be whatever we think it is—but it is not the church. That is, it is not the church in the biblical sense. It is merely an expression of the church.

The title "Pastor" or "Senior Pastor" most commonly identifies the primary leader in a local church congregation. Actually, a better terminology is "Bishop." This is, after all, a much more biblical identifier. But the term bishop has been widely applied to a hierarchical leader within the Catholic Church, or within other specific denominations. An individual with the title of bishop often has authority over a broad range of church congregations and church overseers. In many instances they have the effective position that should be filled by an apostle.

A BROADER PERSPECTIVE

Biblically speaking, the church is comprised of the entire body of believers called out from the world. It is universal—that is, the church is composed of "all who in every place call upon the name of the Lord our God."[1] Beyond that universal concept, the church in the New Testament was regional, comprised of the saints within a city or a region. Local churches, in the sense that we tend to understand them today, are more a development across time than they are a biblical concept. How they evolved into this format is difficult to define or discover.

Perhaps the local church concept came about as various denominations planted church expressions within confined geographical areas. Differing in doctrine, government, and often in relationships, it would have been a natural progression to see more than one congregation within a given locale. In actuality, that probably took place from early on in church history. However, the genesis of the term "local church" is a bit obscure. Nevertheless, it is not a truly biblical terminology.

Today, it is quite common to see congregations gather in such proximity that they share parking facilities. We often see church buildings directly across a street from one another, even when they are part of the same denomination and share common beliefs and core values. And among the small "store-front" churches, it is not uncommon to see two or three congregations meeting within the same complex, at the same time, with different leadership and different agendas.

Most church congregations are small, comprised of less than 100 members. Many have untrained, and all too often, unskilled leadership. Many others meet in homes or small business locations in a burgeoning house church movement. All are somewhat collectively identified as "local churches." This was certainly not the situation in the first century.

THE FIRST CENTURY CHURCH

The church in the first century was notably different. It was not a building, it was a people. It was not primarily an organization, it was organized to accomplish a mission. The first century church was neither democratic nor hierarchical in a governmental sense. Apostolically appointed overseers led it and directed its affairs. It had a council of select elders, and it functioned as a collective within a city,

> THE CHURCH IN THE FIRST CENTURY WAS NOTABLY DIFFERENT. IT WAS NOT A BUILDING, IT WAS A PEOPLE.

a region, or a territory. If we examine the early church closely, we find that it strongly resembled the Jewish religious structure. Many of the Jewish believers continued to pursue temple worship. The Jerusalem church often met within the confines of the temple. And initially, there was no suggestion that the church would embrace or provide for non-Jewish converts.

One must further remember that all of the first apostles were Jews. They grew up in a Jewish society. They were schooled in a synagogue. They were raised under rabbinical concepts, with Jewish cultural understanding. Establishing them as apostles, although it was a totally new concept to religious Judaism, did not erase their Jewish tendencies. Appointing elders made sense to them.

Nothing in the Bible indicates that God desired to tear away those things He had worked in the past. What Jesus did was rip away the fabric of tradition. He exposed the inherent weakness in a religious experience void of a relationship with God. Almost all of the major personalities recorded in the Old Testament Scriptures had experienced an intimate, personal relationship with God—Abraham, Israel, Moses, Joshua, Samuel, and David, just to name a few. The prophets had demonstrated the efficacy of direct and forthright conversation with the Almighty—Ezekiel, Daniel, Isaiah, and Jeremiah. Nothing in the lives of the prophets indicated a need to reconfigure the infrastructure God had established. They did not redesign the culture. So why would Jesus?

The Holy Spirit is the master of using the immediate and available to accomplish His purpose. He does not hesitate based on age or gender or ethnicity or economic advantage. In Him there is neither male nor female, Jew nor gentile, bond nor free.[2]

> THE HOLY SPIRIT IS THE MASTER OF USING THE IMMEDIATE AND AVAILABLE TO ACCOMPLISH HIS PURPOSE.

EARLY CHURCH ORGANIZATIONAL STRUCTURE

Although the Bible does not specifically detail the process, in Acts chapter 6 the apostles appointed those who were approved by the people to be overseers. And the apostle Paul instructed his protégé, Titus, to appoint elders in every city.[3] There was no election, no popular vote, no political positioning. Selection to the responsibility of elder was accomplished by appointment. First, there was a qualification process.[4] Similar qualifications are recorded for the office of bishop.[5] But the apostle in authority made the appointment.

The New Testament office of bishop (Gk. *episkopos*) is far removed from the current usage of the term. Many denominations, beginning with the Roman Catholic Church, use the term to designate an overseer of overseers— someone who has authority over a city or a geographical region. There is no real harm in that, but it was not a New Testament practice. A bishop was an elder, and most likely was the senior elder within a church. He could have been an apostle. However, there is no evidence that it would have been required for him to be one. Actually, the stronger evidence is that bishops and elders were under the influence of apostles. Theirs was the task of overseeing the spiritual life and nurture of the various congregations.

Deacons (Gk. *diakonos*) were also appointed. We surmise that their responsibilities were connected with the details of daily life, with serving and insuring that the growing flock was nurtured. However, we know from Paul's writings that their qualifications positioned them to be ministry leaders far more than simply "table waiters." Quite possibly, people whom Paul would eventually identify as apostles, prophets, evangelists, and teachers once filled the offices of elders and deacons. Certainly the whole concept of "equipping the saints for the work of ministry"[6] fell within the boundaries of their responsibilities. Notably, when the great apostle communicates the qualifications for bishops and deacons,[7] he does so with seemingly no concern for qualifying the lives of "five-fold" ministry gifts. Yet, there must have been some. It is unimaginable that the qualifications on their lives would be less than those on men and women of lesser responsibility.

APOSTOLIC PROMOTION

Many within the contemporary apostolic movement are convinced that apostles, though called by God to be so, grow into their calling. In other words, apostles, like generals or patriarchs, are incapable of fulfilling the role without adequate maturity and significant ministry experience. Second lieutenants do not become generals straightaway. They become first lieutenants. In time, they become captains, then majors. If they endure, they become lt. colonels and then colonels. In the process, they are trained and experienced at growing levels of command. They move from small to large, from simple to complex. They hold minor responsibilities before they are assigned major ones. They become effective at executing commands before they are trusted to give commands to be executed. There is a progression—a factor of maturity, increased knowledge, and the ability to innovate and execute that must be developed.

> **THEY MOVE FROM SMALL TO LARGE, FROM SIMPLE TO COMPLEX.**

Apostolic advance tends to follow a similar progression without a corresponding ranking system. True, there are not lieutenant apostles and general apostles. Still, immature apostles and apostolic leaders should progress from a junior, or less developed status to a more senior, more extensively qualified role with time and experience. Effective apostles tend to develop through a series of skill developing life struggles that mature and strengthen them.

The current cultural climate in which the apostolic community is operating has produced a wide array of impatient young people who want their full allotment immediately. We sometime describe them as the "young guns." They are fervent, impatient, and raring to go forward. In the process, they often disregard and dishonor the very people who paved the way for their success. They sometimes move recklessly and communicate in ways that expose their immaturity, thus revealing their lack of wisdom and their lack of prudence.

In the military, people's lives are at stake. Commanders who are inept create huge problems. They fail to accomplish their objectives, and they occupy places of authority that more competent men and women could fill. In the "army of God" there is little difference. Immature or incompetent leadership results in weak churches and weaker Christians. The development of an effective apostle requires that such an individual have a vast inventory of spiritual, intellectual, and experiential resource in facing the myriad problems, difficulties, and challenges of ministry life. He or she will be directing the efforts of hundreds or thousands of people in achieving the fulfillment of the great commission and the adherence to God's mandate to exercise dominion in the earth.

Patriarchs and matriarchs do not become the respected, honored leaders of a clan without first being children, then adults, then parents. Becoming a grandparent requires years of growth, not only in oneself, but in others also. Your children must grow and mature as well before you can occupy the place of patriarchal influence.

The Importance of the Maturation Process

Our society has tried to accelerate maturation without embracing the necessity of process. It is common preaching to speak about "acceleration." This is true both with and beyond the scope of the church. But, we should use great caution when attempting to hasten maturation. Rapid advancement may well not be God's plan, regardless of our prophetic eagerness to proclaim and reach for the ideal. God is extremely patient and long suffering.

Remember, God allowed approximately four or five thousand years to pass between the fall of mankind and the cross. Jesus slowly and methodically prepared the first apostles for their commissioning, and did not commission them until they were prepared—and they were the first apostles. He has allowed the church to continue for another two thousand years without drawing history to a close. We need to slow down a bit. We need to take the responsibility to righteously, methodically, and with great wisdom, prepare our "young guns" for the rigorous duty they are going to face. They are not generals. They are not patriarchs or matriarchs—at least not yet.

Today, in our society, children are giving birth to children. Parents are becoming grandparents when they are barely mature enough to be parents. I have seen grandmothers who were not yet thirty years of age, charged with raising grandchildren because their own children-parents were still in high school. No one will be a matriarch in those families. They will occupy the position, but they will not be able to provide the mature insight and wisdom that will stabilize the situation.

The patriarchal pattern in the Bible indicates a father over a clan with sons, grandsons and even great grandsons looking to him for wisdom, guidance, and direction. This well serves the pattern for the apostolic, particularly where the apostle is a spiritual patriarch or matriarch. The veneration of such worthy leaders should be significant, to be sure. But, it must also be earned. The children may well understand how to respect the parents, but it is incumbent upon the parent to be respectable. Nothing is more damaging to apostolic community than having an apostle who is incompetent, immature, or dishonorable in the position of leadership.

My dear friend and mentor, John Kelly often describes apostleship as one of, or a combination of three occupations: general, patriarch (or matriarch), and ambassador. I have addressed the first two. Now let me speak to the ambassadorial role of apostleship.

An apostle is a combination of three occupations: general, patriarch (or matriarch), and ambassador.

-John P. Kelly

APOSTLES AS AMBASSADORS

An ambassador is a diplomatic official sent to and positioned within a sovereign government. He or she serves as the official representative of his or her own country. In the case of an apostle serving as an ambassador, he or she is an authorized representative of the Kingdom of God, given to speak for and in response to the will and purposes of the King—Jesus. That ambassador does not exercise authority over the country (sphere) in which they are positioned. They exercise the voice of the Sovereign to that sphere.

> AN AMBASSADOR APOSTLE IS AN AUTHORIZED REPRESENTATIVE OF THE KINGDOM OF GOD— EXERCISING THE VOICE OF THE SOVEREIGN GOD TO THAT SPHERE.

This is quite a different role than being a patriarch or a general. There is no troop to command, no family to protect or nurture. This ambassadorial role is to bring insight, wisdom and encouragement from the King to the one who is responsible over that realm. Whether to a church, a network, a coalition of brethren, or an association of businesses and ministries, the ambassador's authority is to introduce the desires of His Sovereign into the life-flow of that sphere. If accepted, he or she may work to help effect the necessary adjustments for Kingdom advance. Thus, an ambassadorial apostle will communicate what God has directed. But the application and execution of those desires is not his or hers to accomplish. Those are the responsibility of the set leader.

Like the roles of general and patriarch or matriarch, the ambassadorial role, even in world politics, is not given to novices and aspirants. It is given to trusted, loyal men or women of proven character. They must have significant diplomatic skills and be well schooled, both in the desires of their Sovereign and in the workings of the realm to which they are assigned. If they do not, they will usually not be able to accomplish the mission or task they have been assigned to accomplish.

Few apostles are simply one or the other of these three. Usually, they will have some level of responsibility in at least two of the areas. They could be a general and a patriarch, or an ambassador and a general. But whichever role an apostle is delegated to fill, it is always a governmental role, it is always directly connected to the Sovereign Lord's will and command. It is never intended to be operated without His direct guidance and permission.

DISCUSSION QUESTIONS

✦ Discuss the universal or global nature of the church.

✦ Compare the difference that might be seen in the varying roles of apostles as generals, as patriarchs/matriarchs, and as ambassadors.

✦ Can you think of ways that "young guns" could be better developed so that they will be positioned to lead in more effective ways in the future?

✦ Recognizing that you may not fill a five-fold assignment, in which of the apostolic roles do you find yourself most comfortable? Why?

✦ To what degree do you see yourself being "apostled" into your workplace, your community, or your social/cultural environment, and what can you do to be effective in that role?

APOSTLES
FILL A
GOVERNMENTAL
ROLE THAT IS
ALWAYS CONNECTED
TO THE SOVEREIGN
LORD'S WILL AND
COMMAND.

CHAPTER
9

THE APOSTOLIC
COMMUNITY
AT WAR

The apostolic community continuously encounters spiritual warfare. For that matter, so does the entire Christian community. But many Christians, perhaps most of them, are simply unaware of this fact. As long as the church refuses to invade the culture, we can expect that people will continue not to see how intense the warfare really is. Now wait a minute, you might say. We know about Satan and the powers of darkness. We know that Satan is at work against the church and its people.

That is true. Over the past few decades the presence and power of Satan has been acknowledged more and more. In fact, Satan has become the standard excuse for personal weakness, misconduct, and failure. But far too many Christians fail to recognize the effectiveness with which the forces of darkness wage war and the influence they exert on individuals, organizations, ideologies, and nations. The attack against Kingdom people is intense, but it is largely invisible. And because it can't be seen, people often fail to realize it exists. Instead, they give in to a prevailing stream of cultural disintegration that is gripping our families, our communities, our nation, and our society.

One of the crucial issues dominion people face is that Satan lays claim to territory he has no right to possess. In many instances, territory has been yielded by previous generations and the enemy's occupation has grown very strong. In other areas, Satan presses for new ground and Christians too easily yield territory to him that he does not control. In both arenas, the enemy constantly sets distracting influences and deceptions in our pathways. These create confusion over our beliefs, our commitments, our responsibilities, and even our relationships.

UNSPIRITUAL BATTLEGROUNDS OF SPIRITUAL WARFARE

Many are the battles that we engage in with little or no attention to their spiritual implications. Sometimes, seemingly without provocation, tempers become inflamed. Men and women who otherwise are quite stable become destabilized and frustrated. Instead of cooperating, they build walls of defense against one another. Competition rises. Friends become rivals. Brothers and sisters in the Lord become disloyal to one another. They discredit and even denounce one another impulsively, never considering the spiritual impact on someone else's ministry, character or effectiveness. Thus, a very unspiritual conflict generates a very spiritual consequence.

Leaders are often very provincial. This too is a spiritual battleground. Pastors or church leaders stake out territories of personal space, congregational space, or ministry space. They become suspicious, distrusting, and condemning. As a result, they pursue their own interests, often to the detriment of a congregation, a church family, and sometimes creating division in the body of Christ. The world mocks, and Satan laughs.

Instead of being a collection of Kingdom-minded people, such leaders establish their own small kingdoms and distance themselves from those who are different. If there is cooperation in any arena, these leaders are careful not to expose any of their resources or personnel to takeover. After all, in such a contentious atmosphere, someone would surely steal sheep or take away power. Such is the atmosphere in which many churches operate. What can be done? Spiritual warfare is the answer.

THE SPIRITUAL WARFARE WE RECOGNIZE

Spiritual warfare has been categorized into three different groupings—ground level spiritual warfare, occult level spiritual warfare, and strategic level spiritual warfare.

SPIRITUAL WARFARE

GROUND LEVEL

OCCULT LEVEL

STRATEGIC LEVEL

GROUND LEVEL SPIRITUAL WARFARE

The first, ground level spiritual warfare, is focused primarily on struggles with the demonic at the personal level. There is some disagreement about whether or not a person can have a demon. Certainly he can if he wants one. Demons are not very discriminating regarding an individual's profession of faith. They are more than willing to attack anyone, influence their thinking, and diminish their effectiveness.

At this level of spiritual warfare, demons are cast out of (or away from) people's lives so that their influence will no longer control that individual's actions, thoughts, or responses. This is accomplished by a process we call deliverance, and it has proved to be quite effective in establishing personal freedom, particularly when it is followed by the imposition of personal discipline to maintain the deliverance.

OCCULT LEVEL SPIRITUAL WARFARE

The second level is called occult level spiritual warfare. It is also warfare with the demonic, but these spirits are more specifically directed toward ideologies, philosophies, and group structures. The whole arena of the occult is their domain, and they exact a heavy toll on those who adhere to their influence. Some fraternal organizations and orders also demonstrate a high level of occultism, affecting an unsuspecting clientele who have little or no idea that they are being influenced by the demonic. In fact, many who participate in these orders are regular and upstanding members of church congregations and religious institutions. In most cases, they are unsuspecting that their involvement has any impact on their spiritual well being at all. They have been drawn in by friendships, benevolent activities, and social opportunity. Only after being receptive to blood vows, word curses, or sworn allegiance to secretive silence are they even allowed to join such groups.

Occult level spiritual warfare is often waged by revelation. This is particularly true for those in occult influenced organizations. To gain deliverance, an individual who becomes aware of the influence such demonic thinking has held over their lives must disavow the organization and remove themselves completely from its grip. That is hard for some because of the intensity and the power of the vows they have made and the curses they embrace. Though not driven by religious ideologies, ethnic gangs and organized crime families demonstrate the same characteristics. They maintain control with blood vows, word curses, and threats of extreme violence to defectors from their ranks.

Those who practice overt occultism are quite often brought to deliverance through some supernatural event, whereby the power that holds them is superseded by a superior power. In both instances, some level of ground level warfare must follow. The demonic influences to which they have been exposed do not yield territory easily. If at all possible, these demons will return to claim their former place in the lives of the individual, even if that individual never overtly returns to the occult or to an influenced organization.

Strategic Level Spiritual Warfare

Strategic level spiritual warfare is the third grouping connected to spiritual warfare. Properly trained prayer warriors who have been specially equipped for such battles are the ones who should enter such warfare. Strategic level spiritual warfare is demanding. It focuses on territorial spirits—extremely powerful demonic entities which exercise influence over cities, regions, states, nations, or territories.

This kind of warfare requires a more militant approach than most Christians are equipped to enter. An array of warriors, led by spiritual generals and managed by various spiritual leaders in descending orders of authority, collectively engages in these events. Of course, there have been instances where an individual has successfully engaged in a strategic level battle and won. But, it is not common.

> **The objective of strategic level spiritual warfare is to break the spiritual bondage over a territory and destroy the influence of the controlling demonic authority.**

The objective of strategic level spiritual warfare is to break the spiritual bondage over a territory and destroy the influence of the controlling demonic authority. It is vital that the warriors are equipped in such a way that the warfare can be victorious. Such strategic level engagement often calls for the organizational and leadership involvement of a spiritual general in order to be most effective. The collective force of a well-managed army of intercessors is far more powerful than a rag-tag band of spiritual guerrillas.

Generals who command this level of warfare must be strong, mature apostles or prophets, or apostles who are prophets. These individuals have most likely been engaged in the war for a long time and have fought many battles. They have learned the enemy's strategies and tactics and know how to deploy the forces of the Kingdom against them in effective ways. Following the leader is basic discipline for those who are engaged in spiritual disciplines. Those who are unwilling to do so are often little more than cannon fodder for Satan's forces.

GETTING INVOLVED IN SPIRITUAL WARFARE

Spiritual warfare is not for the faint of heart. Neither should it become the focus of a believer who has not powerfully dealt with his or her own carnality. Such negligence usually results in either an ineffectual warfare, or worse, in the capture and destruction of the believer(s) involved.

A call to spiritual warfare is, first of all, a call to personal piety. Now there is a word we don't often use. Piety may best be expressed as a deep and consistent devotion to God, expressed through a sense of authentic reliability. It is holiness experienced more than expressed.

> **PIETY IS HOLINESS EXPERIENCED MORE THAN EXPRESSED.**

Holiness is not an option for any believer. Breaches in holiness open the door to disaster. Demonic powers quickly seize any opportunity that is afforded them. Those who engage in intentional spiritual warfare often stand very close to the fire. No one should enter into this arena of ministry carelessly.

Spiritual warfare, like evangelism, is not optional for the believer. However, we are not all gifted in the same ways. God provides spiritual gifting to each member of the body with a particular assignment in mind. That assignment will define the skill sets and training necessary to fulfill that responsibility. Today, excellent training and guidance are readily available for those who sense that they are specifically called to engage in spiritual warfare. No longer is it a trial and error proposition. Readers who are interested in pursuing this area of life and ministry should research available training venues and submerge themselves in the school of development, discipline, and determination.

PREPARING THE WARRIOR FOR BATTLE

Spiritual warfare is far more than prophetic prayer and intercession. Personal accountability and excellence in character are of vital importance. Personal discipline and victorious relationships are often overlooked as being components of competent warfare, but these too are vital elements of spiritual strength. It is all too easy to challenge every weakness, failure, or shortcoming as a demonic attack. Personal irresponsibility and sin can easily be dismissed as nothing more than a demonic attack, when in reality they are self-inflicted wounds. Spiritual warriors must be adequately prepared to face the challenges and testing that spiritual warfare triggers.

Many times a warrior has been lost to the battle because of friendly fire or a self-inflicted wound. Satan loves this. He loves to have people shift responsibility for their weaknesses and failures onto his shoulders. When that happens, the warrior fails to adjust and grow strong. Those kinds of warriors quickly become "sounding brass and tinkling cymbals." Unable to exercise personal responsibility and accountability, they have little power to confront the enemy successfully. Rest assured

> **MANY TIMES A WARRIOR HAS BEEN LOST TO THE BATTLE BECAUSE OF FRIENDLY FIRE OR A SELF-INFLICTED WOUND.**

that if there is interpersonal conflict between warriors, or personal internal turmoil, the enemy will try to use it to his advantage.

The battle lines are indistinct. They are blurred, fuzzy—out of focus. Some who look like friends quickly become enemies or, if not enemies, stumbling blocks. It is not always easy to distinguish who the enemy is. He is subtle. His demonic cohorts are as well. They seem to like it best when their activities disrupt the peace with their presence being revealed. To do this they have to generate sufficient diversion to get a warrior focused on an external battle. With such noticeable warfare being waged, internal conflict and turmoil is treated as though it were the normal course of life. It is not addressed, and victory is thwarted.

Fallen ministries provide ample evidence of this reality. Broken marriages and unholy alliances do as well. If you compromise with wickedness you open the door to disaster. Ignore the reality of a personal battle or relational conflict and such a battle can quickly consume you. Still, not every breach of holiness produces a conflict. Not every broken spiritual discipline provokes inner turmoil. If they did, people would be more apt to realize the problem and address it.

> IF YOU COMPROMISE WITH WICKEDNESS YOU OPEN THE DOOR TO DISASTER.

What does occur? Defenses are compromised. Vigilance is weakened. The subtle acceptance of gradually elevated levels of evil leaves a warrior vulnerable. Satan will not attack today if he can foresee a growing weakness in an individual. He will bide his time, until the Christian warrior has done significant ministry. Be unrepentant of a sin, or refuse to address a moral weakness, eventually it will come to haunt you. Then you can blame it on the devil, but the real culprit will stare at you from your own mirror. The spiritual war that is lost is the one with the old man.

EVERY CHRISTIAN MUST ENGAGE

No nation dedicates its entire population to military enterprise at any one time. Neither should we who are in God's Kingdom. The Kingdom is complex. It requires us to engage the world on many fronts. Being a soldier, more particularly being engaged in strategic level spiritual warfare, is simply not for everyone. While the whole of the body of Christ is essentially a part of the army of God, we are, first and foremost, the family of God. Christians usually relate more to the familial nature more than they do to being engaged in warfare. However, this does not relieve anyone from doing battle with the enemy.

We may not see ourselves as soldiers, but we are all in the fight. We may not all intercessors, but we must all intercede from time to time. We are not many apostles, but we are all sent into the world with the Great Commission and the mandate to bring dominion into the earth. Being apostolic does not make you an intercessor or a spiritual warrior. It does, however require you to take spiritual warfare seriously and do battle with the enemy effectively for the culture you are in.

> WE ARE SENT INTO THE WORLD, TO ENGAGE THE WORLD AS CITIZENS AND FRIENDS WITH THE LIFE CHANGING GOSPEL OF JESUS CHRIST.

We are sent into the world, to engage the world as citizens and friends with the life changing Gospel of Jesus Christ. We live it out in our daily walk. Our morals, our ethics, our values, and our engagements reflect that reality. We stand under the authority of apostles as the church in the world. We accept the wisdom, direction, and counsel of these God-given gifts to our lives. We follow their leadership, whether it comes from the pulpit as church leaders, from behind the desk as business entrepreneurs, from the classroom as educators, or from the ballet barre as skilled dancers.

Some of us must be in business. Some will be in education. Others must function as leaders in secular government, or influence the media. Many of us will be focused on the family. It is, perhaps, the most overlooked element of our culture and society today. Some of us must lead and administrate the church. If that does not happen, the church will be irrelevant. But, it dare not be. The church is the venue God has chosen to empower everyone for the task He has assigned them. All of us need to be involved, not just in a single area, but in multiple arenas where we develop and grow as Christian disciples, and where we can exert Godly influence on those around us.

Seven specific spheres of culture have been identified as the primary areas that shape and mold a culture. This model was initiated by Loren Cunningham of Youth with a Mission and Bill Bright of Campus Crusade for Christ. Their reasoning was that seven specific cultural areas could be identified in such a way that, if they could be transformed by the message of the Gospel, we could reclaim our culture. These seven areas are currently being presented as the seven mountains of cultural influence. They have also been identified as the mind molders of society. They are listed as;

+ Spirituality & the Church (or Religion)
+ Family
+ Education
+ The Media
+ Government
+ Business
+ Entertainment & the Arts

Each must be warred for. Each must be addressed with a different battle plan and strategy. Each will require a dedicated force of committed and well-trained apostolic Christians to fight the battles for gaining influence. All must be won.

It is important to rehearse the fact that apostolic government extends to every sphere. But these cannot all be addressed from a strictly spiritual point of view. The spiritual realm is primarily intangible. The battles we must fight are usually very tangible and very visible. When we try to define the church only in spiritual or religious ideals, we lose the impact of our strength. The church is indeed spiritual, but it is also very visible and very tangible. People in cultural spheres outside of the church most often do not "get it." But, the church is far more than a building, far more than a religious gathering, organization, or exercise. The church is the epicenter of cultural transformation.

> ## The church is the
> ## epicenter of cultural
> ## transformation.

It is the locus from which Kingdom activity emanates and the command post from which spiritual warfare is administered.

Warfare in the Workplace

Today, those not specifically engaged in church or para-church related employment are considered to be, for want of a better term, "marketplace ministers." A broader term would be "workplace ministries," which is a more inclusive expression that embraces all of the areas of life and activity. I suppose we could specifically identify each area, governmental ministries, educational ministries, etc. However, that would be cumbersome as a way to talk about ministry outside the church infrastructure. So, we will be content to identify them all under the general heading "workplace."

The presence of the Kingdom, the government of the Kingdom, and the power of the Kingdom have an impact on each of them, just as it does over the church. Things become confusing when these areas overlap. What are the protocols? Who has authority in a given situation? Which apostle yields to the other, and when, and for how long? Does the pulpit ministry have authority over the marketplace? Or vice-versa?

Most ecclesiastical leaders believe and assert that they carry the greatest weight in most, if not all, situations. Realistically though, this is not so cut and dried as it may seem. Remember, the defining quality of apostolic leadership is relationship. Apostles lead by influence. They lead by command only in the most extreme of circumstances. True apostolic generals should recognize which among them has the greater effectiveness in a given set of circumstances and yield to that one. An individual's sphere is not threatened when

> **THE DEFINING QUALITY OF APOSTOLIC LEADERSHIP IS RELATIONSHIP. APOSTLES LEAD BY INFLUENCE.**

he yields. Rather, it is strengthened. Usually, when numerous apostles are on scene, an individual leader will, without political positioning, be recognized as the lead voice. Their experience, influence, and relational connectedness to the group will establish them in that position without much difficulty. In turn, they will usually have the intelligence and the wisdom to know when to speak and when to hold their peace. In the process, a lot can be accomplished.

Pulpit leaders need to know their boundaries and limitations, their levels of expertise and experience, and the lack thereof. They must be willing to yield to other leaders in the face of greater insight, wisdom, and skill.

Workplace leaders should also recognize their boundaries. They must know how and when to yield to pulpit leaders and be led in those areas where they are not fulfilling their particular assignments. Every individual Christian needs an overseer. We might call that person pastor, but that person could just as well be an apostle or a prophet. Regardless of title, they will be in a position of spiritual authority and need to be accepted in that role. Furthermore, a person may be under one authority structure in one area of life and ministry and under a completely different one in another area.

Regardless of which mountain or sphere an individual is assigned to, they must be under authority, connected with authority, and committed to authority. Those who are not under authority need to be shunned and their voices quieted by common consent.

When there is con-
tention, posturing or
reaching, no one wins.
When there is a spirit
of cooperation and
collective action, true
leaders know how to
yield to and follow
Godly wisdom. Then
everyone wins.

> **TRUE LEADERS
> KNOW HOW TO
> YIELD TO AND
> FOLLOW GODLY
> WISDOM.**

WARRING WITH PRIDE—
WINNING WITH HUMILITY

Pride is a persistent source of conflict in Christianity. Little wonder then that pride also raises its ugly head within the apostolic movement. Pride precedes destruction and a spirit of pride is a certain precursor to a fall.[1] Moreover, pride places an individual in direct conflict with God.[2] We know beyond any controversy that pride is sin. Yet many of us suffer from pride in one form or another. Insecurity is a seedbed for pride. An insecure Christian resists correction, instruction, accountability, and intimacy. This is true regardless of position, calling, or title. Pride infects apostles and prophets in the same way it does choir members and ball players. No one is immune. Everyone must fight against it.

This, too, is warfare—spiritual warfare. The enemy, however, stares back at you from the mirror. Pride is primarily the result of insecurity. It manifests as arrogance, superiority, aloofness, or haughtiness. It causes leaders to become demanding, self-serving, and over confident. But let an individual leader become secure in their walk with God and pride begins to be replaced by confidence and boldness. Let a leader become secure in their position and that individual will soon reach out to find others with compassion and encouragement. They will also reach out to discover others who can strengthen them so that they will be more effective and productive.

Such leaders will inherently recognize those areas where they lack expertise or knowledge. They will instinctively listen for the voice of wisdom, look for the one who knows, and solicit assistance to improve their ability to achieve God's mandates. Such leaders will graciously yield to others, recognizing that their own spheres of influence will be better developed though humility.

Those who are more prone to talk rather than listen often miss the most significant moments in a conversation. They are so engrossed with their own opinions that they are not open to anything that could generate change or challenge their own limited point of view.

True apostles and apostolic leaders listen. They engage. They lead and they govern, not by lording it over people or by harsh, demanding rule. Rather, they serve. They serve by leading, to be sure, but they serve.

Humility causes leaders to recognize the value and worth in others. In such recognition comes the capacity to serve them with that which only leaders can give effectively. They push those whom they see God elevating up—not down. They encourage. They strengthen. They challenge. They counsel and they give. They give of themselves—their anointing

> **HUMILITY CAUSES LEADERS TO RECOGNIZE THE VALUE AND WORTH IN OTHERS.**

and their substance. They know that no one and nothing can disengage them from the position God has placed them in.

Humbly, without conceit, such leaders embrace their responsibilities and do everything in their power to promote the success of others. They are gifts, given by God to the body. As such, the success and victory of the body of Christ is always at the forefront of their concerns.

DISCUSSION QUESTIONS

✦ What are the three most recognized types of spiritual warfare and what kinds of effort must be expended to achieve success?

✦ Discuss the concepts presented here that much spiritual conflict is overlooked because it occurs through interpersonal relationships, professional confrontations and financial disparities.

✦ What consequences can readily be seen because pride manifests as insecurity?

✦ Discuss humility as a discipline rather than a character trait that only a few possess.

CHAPTER
10

KINGDOM CULTURE IN THE APOSTOLIC COMMUNITY

The Kingdom of God, Jesus said, is like a grain of mustard seed that when planted grows into a mighty tree and the birds of the air find a place for their nests.[1] Could it be that Jesus was predicting something other than what we normally see? Could it be that the radical change of the seed to the full-grown plant is indicative of the dramatic transformation that occurs as the Kingdom grows within a community?

All of the genetic components are present in the seed, but growth produces a transition that is most dramatic.

> **ALL OF THE GENETIC COMPONENTS ARE PRESENT IN THE SEED, BUT GROWTH PRODUCES A TRANSITION THAT IS MOST DRAMATIC.**

Immediately after the seed is planted everything looks the same as it did before it was planted. But growth changes everything. Early on, the growth seems slow and the promise of harvest seems far away. But growth is dynamic. Growth indicates life. Growth comes because the plant is receiving a continuing supply of nutrients. If it is being watered, the plant will absorb the nutrients and fruit will begin to appear. Eventually, the fruit will mature and be available as a food source. It will also be available as seed.

SEEDS OF THE APOSTOLIC

So it is with the apostolic community. When the seeds of the apostolic are planted nothing seems to be different. But as it expands, the apostolic community creates a new domain. It becomes a domain of hope, of excellence, and of refuge—not only for the church, but for the surrounding community as well. At first, the growth seems all too slow. Things don't change fast enough. People don't understand like they should. But, patience is the virtue of the seed planters. They know that the proper nutrients are available. All they need to do is weed, water, fertilize—and wait.

The apostolic seedling has a way of becoming a mighty apostolic tree. Wholly unrelated people quickly find it to be a place of protection, encouragement, and strength. The mighty apostolic tree is filled with fruit that can feed and strengthen all its environs. Moreover, the mature tree has such abundant fruit that it produces many seeds, and the cycle is repeated again and again.

This may not be the popular interpretation of Jesus' parable, but in the light of recent developments and the staggering growth of Christianity around the world, it bears consideration. When apostolic leaders communicate about the role they fulfill, they inevitably turn to God's directive to subdue the earth and rule (govern righteously) over it. That must begin within the body of believers and expand to a lost and dying world.

> **IT CANNOT BE ASSUMED THAT KINGDOM DOMINION WILL SPRING FROM THE WORLD OF BUSINESS.**

It cannot be assumed that Kingdom dominion will spring from the world of business. Jesus never said it would. Education and science will not establish the Kingdom. In fact, these fields have so embraced a non-Kingdom mentality that they have collectively realigned mankind's basic assumptions regarding origins, morality, and life's purposes away from biblical truth.

The imaginations of artists or the fantasies of the silver screen will not release the Kingdom. They have been, in most instances, captivated by a culture wholly opposed to the plan and purpose of God. And most certainly the governments and manipulations of men will not exercise Kingdom dominion unless Godly men and women first fill the positions of power.

THE CHURCH, THE WORKPLACE AND THE PREVAILING CULTURE

Regardless of which particular cultural sphere an individual finds themselves involved in, the rise of ministry in the workplace inevitably and only rises out of the church. The church is the God-established means to captivate and exercise influence over the culture. But the church has not done that effectively. The church has, in most instances, been content to act as a moral addendum to the culture around it. This may seem like a harsh indictment of the church, but it is fairly accurate. Until recently, the church's focus on the society around it has been to draw people into the church, its organization, and its community.

"Come, join us," has been the cry. However, the church has been reluctant to say, "Let us come and join you. Let us come and help you build a better business, a better community, a more honest educational structure or more meaningful art." When we honestly assess our presence within the world around us, we must admit that to a large degree, the Christian community has remained comfortably behind its "stained-glass" wall. The separation of the secular and the sacred has been manifested, not only in our acquiescence to the separation of church

> **THE CHRISTIAN COMMUNITY HAS REMAINED COMFORTABLY BEHIND ITS "STAINED-GLASS" WALL.**

and state, but also to the separation of church and practically everything else. Sadly, the prevailing culture has been more effective in defining the church than the church has in defining the culture.

The apostolic community must find itself opposed to this kind of thinking, and it will. We come into the apostolic with a mindset that has been pre-engineered by our environment, our culture, and our upbringing. That will not necessarily change overnight. Even if we see things differently and understand intellectually that this is true, our natural and unguarded responses will be driven from our past, not our future.

How often have you said recently, "I'm going to church?" or, "Let's go to church?" When you share God's good news with someone, do you invite them to church? What does that mean? Come to our building, to our service, to our world and see what we are about?

How else could we think about it? That's the way the infrastructure of our churches works, and that's the mindset we hold. Not only do Christians think this way, but those who are non-Christians do as well. They also think of the church in church-defined themes. That is why the separation is so tangible.

How would things be if, when a Christian shares the love of Jesus, instead of inviting someone to church, they invite themselves into that person's life? What if they became a part of their world, touched their problems, shared their dreams and cared for their needs? Not exclusively, mind you, but enough so that inviting someone to share in the culture of worship and the friendship of saints would be a natural extension of a developed friendship instead of an evangelistic outreach. Would that be different?

When you read the New Testament without "stained glass" lenses, particularly the book of Acts, you quickly see that those early Christians were not about building the next mega-church worship center or a strong religiously oriented entertainment event. They were genuinely interested in people. They were willing to spend and be spent so that the Gospel of Jesus Christ could become part and parcel of the lives of the people they touched. The first Christians made disciples before they built congregations. That was, and is, the nature of the apostolic. It is engaged with the society around it. It is Kingdom, and it is dominion.

> **THE FIRST CHRISTIANS MADE DISCIPLES BEFORE THEY BUILT CONGREGATIONS.**

BEING APOSTOLIC—THE METHODS OF THE EARLY CHURCH

The office of apostle is strategically important as the governing role within the culture of the church. It is because of this role that we dare call the movement apostolic. Being apostolic does not mean that a person is an apostle. It means that they are a part of a Christian expression that is governed strategically by apostles and committed to the process of dominion. The term 'apostle' was the first nomenclature Jesus used to identify individuals who would specifically be set in position to direct the development of church life.

These apostles were the men who became the immediate overseers of the church, from the day of Pentecost in Acts 2 until the office passed into neglect. They were selected and trained for more than three years before they were left in position to function on their own. When the church was birthed, these twelve men were uniquely prepared for the moment. Their immediate disciples were so empowered that they were noted to "have turned the world upside down."[2] These apostles (along with a beginning team of 120 believers) with dynamic courage, supernatural anointing, and a willingness to oppose, confront, and engage the cultural, political, social, and religious structures around them, formed the early church.

Apart from the office of apostle, other ministerial offices were not recognized or identified until after the church was formed and active. True, the concept of a prophet had lingered from Old Testament times, for prophets of old had been a significant part of the religion of the Hebrews. But let us not forget, the last Old Testament prophet was Malachi. Prophets (or prophetic people) were part of the spiritual landscape.

Four hundred years of prophetic silence preceded the coming of Jesus and the establishment of the New Covenant. We have no biblical record of prophetic ministry between the Testaments. A variety of spiritual writings from this period did receive acceptance as Scripture by some segments of the church. However, these are in dispute, especially among those of us known as Protestants, Evangelicals, Pentecostals, and Independents. Those books are called the Apocrypha and are found primarily in Roman Catholic translations of Scripture. Nevertheless, we do find prophets in the New Testament.

At His dedication, a devout man named Simeon prophesied over Jesus.[3] The first recorded prophet in the New Testament was an obscure woman named Anna. She left no recorded words, only the legacy that she spoke about this child to all who were looking for the redemption of Israel.[4] These instances serve to validate the revelation God gave to Amos hundreds of years earlier. "Surely the Sovereign Lord does nothing without revealing His plan to His servants the prophets."[5]

As a result, if there were any known prophetic models during that time, they had no impact on the development, delivery, or recording of Holy Writ. The closest thing to a prophetic voice that the New Testament prophets had, prior to the book of Acts, was the voice of John the Baptist, and he was more the model of the evangelist than the prophet. He lived an ascetic lifestyle and dressed in distinctively prophetic garb. He did prophesy, to be sure, and that tends to strengthen his image as a prophet. Perhaps if more evangelists were more prophetic, the impact of evangelism would be more strongly felt across the land.

The understanding of the ministries of pastors and teachers could easily have been derived from the framework of the Jewish faith. Priests and Levites performed the sacerdotal duties of the temple. Scribes and teachers of the law (rabbis) provided the education of religious Jews. They were the primary leadership in synagogues and Hebrew schools where boys learned the lessons of faith. Except for the emergence of apostles and New Testament prophets, the church might well have been little more than a reconstruction of other forms of religious worship.

A NEW NATION—THE KINGDOM MANIFESTED

The early church was a collectively empowered new nation, led by divinely appointed emissaries of God, and it rocked the world. Unfortunately, with the decline of the apostolic, the church became just another religious expression. Its apostolic character was lost. A priesthood was established to act as mediators of grace—receiving confession, dispensing forgiveness, donning clerical vestments, and offering sacrifice on behalf of people.

> THE EARLY CHURCH WAS A COLLECTIVELY EMPOWERED NEW NATION, LED BY DIVINELY APPOINTED EMISSARIES OF GOD.

This is the format for worship as it was developed within the Catholic Church and its system of a repetitive sacrifice of Corpus Christi, the body of Christ. This was also far removed from the primitive church of New Testament times. The Genesis church was established by apostles, led by apostles and prophets, and functioned without all of the religious paraphernalia and "foofaraw" found in most churches today. Extravagant additions to early Christian simplicity are not limited to the liturgical community and "high church." Contemporary worship patterns, "feel good" communications, and modern technology can easily be substituted for true intimacy and redemptive, restorative preaching. Big screens and self-serve kiosks can easily replace life-giving hospitality and genuine fellowship.

The early church was a fountainhead of closely held friendship and covenant brotherhood. There was an almost ethnic quality among believers, a unique brotherhood of agapé love. Not only that, but the early church had a profound allegiance to the apostolic leadership and their teachings. The importance of apostles and prophets was foundational to the development of the early church.[6] It is no less so today. The question that exists is this: Why are apostles and prophets so important?

> **WHY ARE APOSTLES AND PROPHETS SO IMPORTANT?**

Apostles and prophets are God's agents equipped to provoke, institute, and project cultural change. They have both the anointing and the gifting to communicate the greater vision of God, and to explain it. They are the designated, appointed overseers of the Kingdom of God, the nation (Gk. *ethnos*) of believers. Apostles and prophets have been placed within the church as foundational offices.[7]

Apostles and prophets are the primary delegates of cultural change, unveiling vision and directing the development of community. Apostles have remarkable authority, both in the natural realm and in the spiritual realm. That authority allows them to influence the core values of people, especially as those people function in a faith context. Their concern is not primarily to adjust or change the national, ethnic, or geographical nature of people, it is to adjust the religious perspective and develop the intrinsic culture of the Kingdom within the hearts and minds of people. The unfolding of vision, the advance of the Kingdom, and the raising up of spiritual sons and daughters are all relevant interests to apostles.

Apostles are men and women of war—not of physical war, but of spiritual war. They are, in essence, spiritual field commanders. Their interests lie, not so much in organizational structure, as in operational strategy. Unless the Lord builds the house, those who build do so in vain.[8] It is the responsibility of the apostles to influence the laborers who build, and to build with them so that their labor has a direct and distinct impact on the immediate community.

Beyond that, through an array of interconnected relationships, they have influence on a global scale.

WORKPLACE MINISTRY
AND THE APOSTOLIC

The rise of Workplace Ministry has given rise to a concept that, while attractive, is not biblical. That does not of itself make it wrong. There just seems to be no biblical evidence to support it. That is the concept of a five-fold ministry in the workplace. The New Testament offers no manifestation of the five-fold offices within the marketplace, only within the church. Yet today, many people teach, and I too have suggested, that these things can be seen in the workplace. Indeed they can.

As have others, I have at times compared the five-fold to a business environment. In this model the apostle functions as CEO, the prophet as market analyst, the evangelist as director of sales, the teacher as training officer, and the pastor as floor manager. It looks good in a business context, but becomes much less evident in other spheres we call workplace, like education and the arts. That does not mean there are no apostles or prophets in the workplace. There are. Apostles and prophets are firmly entrenched throughout the workplace.

Their role is to do business, to educate, to govern, and to fulfill whatever responsibilities their professions require. They do these things with integrity, with dignity, and with honor. But, they do so much more. They lead, and thereby exercise the power of dominion. These workplace ministers use their anointing and ministry skills as tools to influence their environment for righteousness. They elevate productivity and foster success, thus creating a level of credibility and perspective that gives them voice. These powerful Christians in the workplace carry the weight and calling, and ideally the recognition, within the church that goes with a five-fold office. These offices, however, are not workplace offices. They are church offices—or more specifically, Kingdom offices.

Earlier in this book I strongly suggested that the five-fold gifts are not given to individuals, per se, they are individuals given to the church. I also clarified that they are a composite of an individual's particular gifts and skill sets, personality, character, and maturity. Why, then, would this be different for leaders whose primary field is in a workplace environment? It would not.

The prevailing mindset of people has been that ministry is primarily (1) allocated to the church, (2) religious in nature, and (3) something that "flows" down from the pulpit and the platform or altar, in descending order, to ever diminishing levels of ministry importance and responsibility. It continues then that ministry flows out of the doors of the church infrastructure into the highways and byways of life with the sole purpose of returning to the church. Thus, the lost and needy are drawn to the church, inside the protection of the "stained glass wall" to receive ministry.

Most of our "services" are times of pulpit to pew communication. Many of our focuses are times to "invite the lost" to come and hope they will get saved. In a church environment, most of the people who come to the Lord do so at the end of a worship gathering when an invitation or an "altar call" is given. These are norms of church behavior that have, and continue to, affect our thinking. Most prophecies are given "in church." And most of them, at some level, endorse our "church-centered" mentalities.

> **MATURE, APOSTOLIC CHRISTIANS WHO ARE CALLED TO THE WORKPLACE ARE COMMITTED TO THE TRANSFORMATION OF CULTURE AND TO THE EXPANSION OF THE KINGDOM.**

The mature apostolic community cannot function this way. Those whose life calling and responsibility is in the workplace must function in the workplace. If they attempt to function in the same way in the church, they will become an obstruction to the ongoing life and function of the church. They are not necessarily called to function as church officials, they are sent into the workplace as Christians, committed to the transformation of culture and the expansion of the Kingdom. That does not mean they do not or cannot fill a church-related assignment.

They can, and often do. But their primary calling and position is in the workplace, not the church.

Apostles and prophets such as these are not usually ecclesiastical apostles or prophets, not in the sense of being the practicing, full-time overseers and employees of church and para-church activity. If they are called and commissioned as five-fold ministers, that commissioning should be accomplished in the church. Their allegiance and spiritual accountability may well be to the church, or more likely to a recognized, established, and influential apostle. But their primary function is to be commissioned workplace leaders. Their responsibility will be to equip the church[9] with the distinct challenge of raising up saints to effectively minister (make disciples) in their own particular spheres of life.

Business leaders will equip people for business with biblical morals, Godly ethics, and righteous strategies. Educational leaders will equip people to improve education, restore honesty to the classroom, and validate truth. Government leaders will encourage and mentor the development of lawyers, politicians, and military leadership,

> **FIVE-FOLD LEADERS IN A WORKPLACE CONTEXT WILL EQUIP OTHER WORKPLACE PEOPLE IN KINGDOM VALUES, PRODUCTIVITY AND EFFECTIVENESS.**

so that there is an overshadowing environment of justice and peace in the land. In other words, five-fold leaders in a workplace context will equip other workplace people in Kingdom values, productivity and effectiveness.

The growth of the Kingdom in the world is more dependent on the people of God taking The Life to the world than it is in bringing the world to the church to discover The Life. The New Testament pattern is clearly directed to that end. The apostolic structure is clearly focused toward that as a goal. The Great Commission (Matthew 28:19-20) specifically charges us to make disciples—not to make church members. And the Dominion Mandate (Genesis 1:26-28) is a direct command that we must embrace to subdue the earth and its environs—including Satan and the legions of darkness, and exercise dominion.

> **THE GREAT COMMISSION CHARGES US TO MAKE DISCIPLES— NOT TO MAKE CHURCH MEMBERS.**

When we think that this will be accomplished within the infrastructure of the church, we miss the point. The church is not the Kingdom. The church is the epicenter of Kingdom activity. It is also the training center for Kingdom activity. The church is made up of a vast collection of resource personnel whom God has directed to accomplish His purposes in the earth. It must remain in flux, ever adapting to the challenges and opportunities it faces. Its message must remain constant, and its relationship to Jesus undiminished. Unfortunately, in many cases, its means and methods have fallen short of its potential. Restoration is needed, and restoration is taking place. That restoration is a return to an apostolic stance in a 21st century setting. Above all, it is a return to the passion and power of the church's earliest days.

The church is not the Kingdom, but its activities must be concentrated on Kingdom advancement. Furthermore, the Kingdom will not be fully manifested unless and until the church accepts and implements an apostolic composition. That was its original design, the one Jesus instituted and the one He promised to build—and that is what He seems committed to build.

The Kingdom is unchanging. Jesus established it, manifesting it in a temporal world but with eternal purpose. But while the Kingdom remained a constant, the historical church changed. Actually, it has never ceased changing. Gradually, sometimes grudgingly, the church has been pushed and pulled, and prodded. All the time, the Good News of Jesus Christ, His redeeming grace, and His forgiving love has never diminished, never waned. The Truth stands firm.

> **THE KINGDOM IS UNCHANGING.**
>
> **THE CHURCH HAS NEVER CEASED CHANGING.**

> **WHEREVER THE CHURCH IS UNWILLING TO EMBRACE AND ACCEPT CHANGE, IT WILL ULTIMATELY STAGNATE AND DECAY.**

But now, the church must change some more. Now it must return to its apostolic root system, embrace the functional framework that Jesus established, and once again become a dominant force in the world. Wherever the church is unwilling to embrace and accept such change, it will ultimately stagnate and decay. It may look glamorous and successful. It may clothe itself in lavish structures and proclaim its relevance in bold and dramatic terms, but it will only be an empty shell.

This time, the stained glass must be shattered—not literally—but the barriers must come down. The separation between the spiritual and the secular must be dissolved. Clergy will need to redefine their roles while protecting and promoting the church. And they will have to yield their "holy man" status to practical apostolic expansion. Laity, the people of the church, will have to step up to a greater capacity of ministry and refuse to venerate mere men or women beyond their true selves. Honor them, respect them, provide for their well being, yes—but recognize that they are really no different from you and me.

In the final analysis, there is little we can do, unless we are willing to embrace the call to restoration. If we do not do so, the church's influence will continue to wane. Unless the church truly becomes the church manifested within the workplace, among the lost and in the world, it will continue to cower behind a stained glass wall of isolation, spiritual superiority, and ineffectiveness. We will not reverse the trends of society unless we do it God's way.

We must make the turn, return to, and embrace both the apostolic nature and structure the church once knew. I pray that you already have done so. I pray that deep within, you too have developed a passionate desire for effective transformation in your world. Dominion—influencing our world with God's loving reign—is our heritage, our inheritance, and our present opportunity. We can make a real difference, and we must. I pray that your influence will affect a host of others to embrace the call, exercise dominion in your part of the earth, and make disciples.

DISCUSSION QUESTIONS

✦ Discuss the differing nature of apostles and prophets as church and congregational leaders as opposed to those who are called into a workplace setting.

✦ What are the primary responsibilities and biblical tasks of apostles?

✦ Discuss ways that apostles and prophets can advance the Kingdom by accomplishing these tasks.

✦ What areas of pride do you recognize in your own life and ministry and what could you do to adjust it?

BIBLICAL REFERENCES BY CHAPTER

Chapter 1

    1. Luke 5:37-39

    2. 1 Cor. 5:6-8

    3. 1 Cor. 4:6-7

    4. John 21:17

    5. 1 Cor. 4:16; 11:1 KJV

    6. 1 Pet. 2:21-22

Chapter 2

    1. Col. 1:16-17

    2. Ps. 18:30

    3. Acts 4:32-34

    4. Acts 5:1-11

    5. Acts 6:1-6

    6. Acts 8:1-4

    7. Matt. 28:19-20

CHAPTER 3

1. Deut. 12:1-9
2. Col. 1:13-14
3. 2 Peter 1:2-4
4. Eph. 4:11-13
5. John 3:36
6. John 17:4; 19:30
7. John 1:12-13
8. Rom. 8:16-17

CHAPTER 5

1. Acts 2:1-39
2. Acts 2:42
3. John 15:20
4. Acts 2:8-11
5. Acts 6:1-7
6. Acts 8:1-4
7. Acts 8:1-9:31
8. Acts 15:1-29
9. Acts 20:28
10. Heb. 3:1
11. Eph. 4:11-12; 1 Cor 12:28
12. Note Psalm 103:17-19
13. Matt. 16:18
14. Eph 4:8

CHAPTER 7

1. Romans 14:17
2. 1 Tim. 5:22
3. 1 Tim. 3:1-6
4. Lev. 19:32; Prov. 16:31
5. Gal. 1:15-18
6. John 20:19-22
7. Matt. 20:25-28
8. 1 Cor. 14:31
9. Matt. 5:13-14; Luke 14:34-35

CHAPTER 8

1. 1 Cor. 1:2
2. Gal. 3:26-29
3. Titus 1:5
4. Titus 1:6-8
5. 1 Tim. 3:1-7
6. Eph. 4:12-13
7. 1 Tim. 3:1-11; Titus 1:7-9

CHAPTER 9

1. Prov. 16:18
2. James 4:6

CHAPTER 10

1. Matt. 13:31-32
2. Acts 17:6
3. Luke 2:34-35
4. Luke 2:36-38
5. Amos 3:7
6. Eph. 2:19-20
7. Ibid.
8. Psalm 127:1
9. Eph. 4:11-13

ABOUT THE AUTHOR

PHILIP R. BYLER represents the sixth generation of his family to embrace vocational ministry. For more than thirty-five years he has served the Christian community as an apostle, a pastor, and a pioneer in the apostolic movement. Dr. Byler is a seasoned writer and speaker, who has taken the apostolic message around the world. He is the Executive Director of STAR (Strategically Targeted Apostolic Resourcing) Christian Network, headquartered in Atlanta. Dr. Byler serves as a member of the Advisory Council of the International Christian WealthBuilders℠ Foundation (ICWBF).

As Founder and Director of C.T.T.M. Ministries International, Dr. Phil is committed to Coaching, Teaching, Training, and Mentoring emerging apostles, pastors, and ministry leaders. He is dedicated to assisting churches transition into apostolic life, and his message is firmly set against a separation between the sacred and the secular. As a veteran leader within the nuclear church, Philip brings the perspective of an insider to the development of effective ministry outside the boundaries of church infrastructure and to the growing workplace ministry movement.

Philip holds a Doctor of Religious Education degree from Chesapeake Bible College & Seminary. Through the course of his life, he has developed college-level curriculum ranging from Homiletics and Hermeneutics to Church

History and the Book of Revelation. He has taught Greek and is a life-long student and scholar. Phil has planted churches in Georgia, Pennsylvania, and Maryland, discipling and releasing effective leaders in the Kingdom. Dr. Byler travels extensively in the United States and has ministered in Ukraine, Germany, Croatia, Bosnia-Herzegovina, India, Sri Lanka, Japan, Canada, Mexico, Australia and the Bahamas.

Married for over four decades, Phil's wife, Judy, has been a constant companion, supporter, and ministry partner. She holds a Doctor of Pastoral Counseling degree and is a certified counselor with the State of Georgia. She has served as a contract counselor for the Department of Juvenile Justice, counseling at-risk youth from three counties. She is an excellent Bible teacher in her own right, and has a passion to unlock the powerful and insightful truths presented in the Old Testament.

Together they have two married children and seven grandchildren. Their son, Timothy carries on the rich heritage, unbroken as the seventh generation minister in the Byler line. He and his wife, Cindy, pastor Bethesda Church in Hinesville, Georgia, and have four children.

Their daughter and son-in-law, Wendy and Todd Walters, own Palm Tree Productions, a successful media services company located in Keller, Texas. They have three children.

The Bylers reside in a suburb of Atlanta, Georgia.